ARCHITECTING
THE CLOUD

Founded in 1807, John Wiley & Sons is the oldest independent publishing company in the United States. With offices in North America, Europe, Asia, and Australia, Wiley is globally committed to developing and marketing print and electronic products and services for our customers' professional and personal knowledge and understanding.

The Wiley CIO series provides information, tools, and insights to IT executives and managers. The products in this series cover a wide range of topics that supply strategic and implementation guidance on the latest technology trends, leadership, and emerging best practices.

Titles in the Wiley CIO series include:

Transforming IT Culture: How to Use Social Intelligence, Human Factors, and Collaboration to Create an IT Department That Outperforms by Frank Wander

Unleashing the Power of IT: Bringing People, Business, and Technology Together by Dan Roberts

The U.S. Technology Skills Gap: What Every Technology Executive Must Know to Save America's Future by Gary J. Beach

Architecting the Cloud: Design Decisions for Cloud Computing Service Models (SaaS, PaaS, and IaaS) by Michael Kavis

ARCHITECTING THE CLOUD

DESIGN DECISIONS FOR CLOUD COMPUTING
SERVICE MODELS (SaaS, PaaS, AND IaaS)

Michael Kavis

I dedicate this book to my parents, John and Deme, and my brother, Bill, whose work ethic and drive to be the best in their fields serve as inspiration for me to excel and fully embrace my field of computer science.

CONTENTS

FOREWORD

I first met Mike Kavis when he brought our *Licensed ZapThink Architect* SOA course to his company in Florida several years ago. As the vice president of architecture for this firm, Mike hoped to wrangle his group of developers to help them think like architects. And while I couldn't transform developers into architects in four days, the thrust of the course was to help people *think like architects*.

The book you have in your hands now has the same mission. Cloud computing as an approach to IT infrastructure is still emerging, and thus the technical details are still in flux—but the architectural principles of the cloud are now falling into place. But only by thinking like an architect will you be able to take advantage of the full power of the cloud.

Architects are in a unique position in the IT shop, because they have one foot in the business and the other squarely ensconced in the technology. They must understand the nuts and bolts of what works and what doesn't without falling victim to the techie tunnel vision that inflicts so many IT people. But they must also live and breathe the business: its strategy, its goals, and most importantly, its problems.

Architecting the Cloud connects these dots. Mike Kavis has intentionally avoided product- or vendor-specific details, focusing instead on the challenges that architects, as well as stakeholders in the architecture, should address—in other words, connecting the business problem with the appropriate solution. A truism to be sure, but easier said than done in the cloud.

The reason that solving business challenges in the cloud is so difficult is because the cloud is not just one thing. It is many diverse things: SaaS, PaaS, and IaaS service models, public, private, and hybrid deployment models, not to mention diverse value propositions. Some organizations seek to save money with the cloud while others want to shift capital to operational expense. On top of these benefits is elasticity: dealing better with unpredictable demand for IT resources.

Never before has architecture mattered so much. Building *working* solutions in the cloud that *actually address the business need* depends upon it. With his hands-on experience architecting such cloud solutions, Mike Kavis has the experience and insight to lead the way.

—JASON BLOOMBERG
President, ZapThink

PREFACE

If you don't know where you are going,
any road will take you there.
— LEWIS CARROLL, *ALICE IN WONDERLAND*

In the summer of 2008, after three decades of building software in corporate data centers, I walked away from corporate America to take a stab at building a technology company from the ground up based on a clever concept of the start-up company's founder. After years of building software within the constraints of existing data centers and the long procurement cycles required to make new computing resources available to build on, I saw leveraging cloud computing as an opportunity to achieve far greater agility at a pay-as-you-go utility pricing model. When I started my journey I tweeted to my social network and asked if anyone knew of any real-life examples of real-time transaction processing occurring in the public cloud. My tweet generated a lot of laughs and snarky comments; after all, who would have thought of processing information from a brick-and-mortar retail point-of-sale system over the Internet with a transaction engine in the public cloud in 2008? One responder laughed and said, "Let me know when you find an example." It was clear to me that we were pioneers, and we would have to learn things the way pioneers learned: by trial and error. Now, five years later, I want to share my lessons learned with readers so they can rely more on the experiences of others rather than brute force trial and error, like pioneers.

There are many books that define what cloud computing is and how the cloud is the biggest game changer since the rise of the Internet and the birth of the personal computer. The books in the marketplace today typically target management, beginners, or developers. This book is targeting chief technology officers, enterprise architects, product managers, and key technology decision makers.

Several books that target cloud architects get very specific about how to build software in the cloud and often focus on leading vendors. The content within this book is vendor agnostic since all the concepts discussed can be applied to any vendor or proprietary solution. I believe that one of the most critical technology decisions for succeeding with cloud computing is selecting the right cloud service model(s), which should be based on a combination of business, technology, and organizational requirements. Unfortunately, there is a notable absence of information in the marketplace to guide decision makers through this critical decision point. This book is focused on filling that information gap by providing decision makers with the pros and cons of each service model from the viewpoint of a consumer of cloud services.

This book is a must-read for any decision maker starting the vendor selection and development process for their cloud computing initiative. Starting a cloud initiative with a blank sheet of paper is a daunting task. This book provides the reader with an arsenal of design decisions to contemplate and highlights critical areas of concern that all cloud architectures must contend with.

Overview of the Contents

Within each chapter I'll share a story that is relevant to the topic of discussion. These stories are either a personal experience that I have been involved in during my career or one of a peer or colleague. The names of companies, individuals, and products will be masked by fictitious names. Storytelling helps readers relate better to technical topics because we all have similar experiences throughout our careers. As with any other shift in technology, there is a lot of hype and many myths and misperceptions about cloud computing that lead to resistance or difficulties for some organizations in adopting the cloud. I have observed the same behavior numerous times in my career with the adoption of the Internet, service-oriented architecture (SOA), agile methodologies, and others. I have been fortunate enough to have multiple opportunities to be a pioneer for several of these technology shifts. I will use some stories from the past to show the parallels between the resistance to cloud computing and the resistance to the predecessor technologies.

I have always found that discussing technology in terms of familiar business scenarios helps readers to visualize concepts and makes it easier to translate those visualizations to the reader's real-life scenarios. I have created a fictitious online auction company called Acme eAuctions (AEA) and will use AEA to describe many relevant business scenarios to help explain key points throughout this book. I will be discussing many facets of AEA's business, not just its online auction website, so those readers not in the web business need not be alarmed. There will be plenty of scenarios that address relevant business scenarios for all readers.

As You Begin

Architecting the Cloud was written to fill a void that existed when I started building my first cloud application back in 2008. Each chapter provides insights gained through my experiences, both things I got right and things I got wrong. My hope is that by sharing these experiences and providing a list of design considerations in a variety of areas of concern, my readers can make more precise design decisions and will not have to rely as much on trial and error as I did when I first started. Cloud computing can offer tremendous benefits such as increased speed to market, lower total cost of ownership, and greater flexibility if designed correctly, but there are no silver bullets. To achieve these benefits, a pragmatic approach is required. This book aims to arm the reader with a long list of design considerations to help the reader achieve the goals that the cloud promises.

ACKNOWLEDGMENTS

First and foremost, I would like to thank my wife, Eleni, and my kids, Yanni and Athena. They have supported me throughout my career and have made way too many sacrifices over the last decade as my journey took me from four years of graduate studies at night, to five years of being a road warrior, and to the six months when I was holed up in my office writing this book.

I could not have written this book without the guidance, constructive criticism, and encouragement of my friend, mentor, and fellow RESTafarian, Jason Bloomberg, president of ZapThink. Thanks for reviewing my chapters and helping me out at times when I was stuck.

A special thanks goes out to two warriors whom I have taken to battle with me for well over 10 years and who were a major reason we won the AWS Start-Up Challenge in 2010, Greg Rapp and Jack Hickman. Without talented, dedicated, and loyal technicians like these two guys, I would never have gained the experience required to write about the cloud. Nobody was crazy enough to take point-of-sale (POS) transactions out of grocery stores and into the public cloud back in 2008. We were met with resistance from retailers, POS vendors, investors, peers, and just about everyone. Greg and Jack never questioned the strategy and accepted the challenge. Together we changed the retail industry forever, and now cloud-based POS transactions are the future. Thanks, Greg and Jack!

And finally, thanks to my parents for raising me to be driven to be the best I can be. Mom and Dad, just look at the pictures because you won't understand a word of this book.

ABOUT THE AUTHOR

Mike Kavis is a vice president and principal architect at Cloud Technology Partners and an industry analyst. He has served in technical roles such as chief technology officer, chief architect, and vice president positions with over 25 years of experience building enterprise solutions in health care, retail, manufacturing, and loyalty marketing industries.

In 2010, as chief technology officer for start-up M-Dot Network, his company won the prestigious Amazon AWS Global Start-Up Challenge. M-Dot built a high-speed micropayments network that processed digital incentives by integrating brick-and-mortar point-of-sale systems into a digital incentive PaaS built entirely on Amazon's AWS public cloud. M-Dot Network was acquired in 2011. In his spare time he works with several start-ups in an advisory role focusing on architecture and cloud computing. When he is not staring at his computer he enjoys traveling to MetLife Stadium in New Jersey to watch his beloved New York Giants.

CHAPTER 1

Why Cloud, Why Now?

There was a time when every household, town, farm, or village had its own water well. Today, shared public utilities give us access to clean water by simply turning on the tap; cloud computing works in a similar fashion. Just like water from the tap in your kitchen, cloud computing services can be turned on or off quickly as needed. Like at the water company, there is a team of dedicated professionals making sure the service provided is safe, secure, and available on a 24/7 basis. When the tap isn't on, not only are you saving water, but you aren't paying for resources you don't currently need.

—VIVEK KUNDRA, FORMER FEDERAL CIO, U.S. GOVERNMENT

In 2009, I was invited to the IBM Impact conference in Las Vegas as a guest blogger and analyst. *Cloud computing* was a vastly misunderstood term at that time, and there were very few enterprises leveraging any cloud services other than a few of the mature SaaS solutions like Salesforce.com and Concur's expense management software. I witnessed some very intelligent senior IT people from various companies scoffing at the term *cloud computing*. I can still hear the lines: "We were doing this on the mainframe in the '60s" and "There is nothing new here, this is just a fad." At that time, my team of one developer was testing a prototype that was executing hundreds of thousands concurrent point-of-sale (POS) transactions to the cloud and back in subsecond response time on a virtual cloud server, costing us about half a dollar an hour charged against my CEO's credit card. I started to think about how much it would cost to implement the infrastructure, licenses, and professional services to perform a proof-of-concept on-premises. I also thought about how many months it would take to go through a vendor evaluation, the procurement process, and all of the steps required to make a capital expenditure that would have been required to buy servers from a large vendor like IBM. At the end of several months, I would finally have all the hardware, software, licenses, and professional services that my developer would need to test his proof-of-concept. My start-up would have been out of cash by then, and all I would have to show for it would have been a few lunches paid for and a nice golf shirt with the vendor's logo on it.

Instead of doing things as if we were a large company with all the time and money in the world, my team embraced the cloud and saw it as a competitive advantage. Our competition was two to three years ahead of us, but we felt we could provide superior products and services at a price point that could not be matched by companies that were purchasing and managing infrastructure and data centers. My developer was able to provision many different-size servers and test multiple configurations until he finally found the sweet spot. Our cloud services provider, Amazon Web Services (AWS), had made infrastructure management easy by abstracting out all of the complexities into a few simple application programming interfaces (APIs). We could build and deploy numerous server configurations in minutes and de-provision them when we were done. That is a drastic change from days past. Before cloud computing, the thought of asking one's boss to purchase three different types and sizes of servers in order to run a series of tests and theories on them to determine which one is actually the right one was not a feasible or career-enhancing proposition. Buying many different hardware configurations, tossing out the configurations that did not perform optimally, and then going back to procurement to buy more of the right configuration is an insane approach when dealing with physical machines. In the cloud, this is a best practice. Cloud computing resources follow a pay-as-you-go pricing model just like electricity and water. It is easy to test multiple configurations in a prototyping environment with very little investment.

Going back to my example, we used a simple management console to launch numerous virtual computing resources that were ready to run in five minutes. We would run our tests for two hours and then discard the virtual computing resources. Our total cost was 50 cents an hour or $1 worth of infrastructure to run this prototype. Then we would move on to the next server configuration and try another series of tests. We would do this three times during the day and rack up $3 in infrastructure costs. Here is a comparison of prototyping in the cloud versus prototyping in the same manner on-premises:

- **Scenario A (on-premises).** Buy three different severs at roughly $3,000 to $5,000 each, plus software, shipping, and installation.
    - Elapsed time to procure and implement likely to range between one and three months.
    - Outcome: Decide on which server to keep, buy more, get rid of the other two.
- **Scenario B (cloud model).** Developer creates three different virtual computing resources within minutes at $0.50/hour, using one at a time for two hours each (total $3.00).
    - Complete testing and make a decision in one day.
    - Outcome: Complete the entire scenario in one day of work for just $3.00 plus one person's salary. No wasted assets.

That is just one real-life example that made me a believer in cloud computing. As we continued our journey as an early stage start-up I was continually amazed at how quickly we could get work done at such a low cost. We owned no hardware and leveraged open source software. Since we did not have to manage data centers and physical infrastructure, we were able to focus on building product to generate revenue so that our start-up could live to see another day.

Evolution of Cloud Computing

My first job out of college in 1988 was a COBOL programmer working at a steel plant in the South. We were migrating from an old Burroughs mainframe computer to a new IBM 3090 mainframe, which, to put things in perspective of the level of coolness in today's terms, is the equivalent of moving from a feature phone to a smart phone. The code of the first program I worked on was written the year I was born. It had been ported from one mainframe system to the next and was 23 years old at the time. When that code was written, a lot of engineering went into breaking up messages into very small chunks of memory because of mainframe memory limitations in the 1960s. Here we were in 1988 with this then-massive IBM mainframe with what seemed like endless amounts of memory and using code that was working really hard to break things down into 8K chunks. I thought this was absurd, but as a 23-year-old rookie, I shook my head and ported that code to the new system. Little did I know that some 25 years later, masses of people would be taking that same approach as they began porting their legacy applications to the cloud without even considering that the new target environment is drastically different and more powerful than the environment the legacy code is running on. We will discuss stories like this in Chapter 3 ("Cloud Computing Worst Practices").

Cloud computing is the result of many years of evolution dating back to the first computers. It is the natural progression from the centralized mainframe era, to the distributed client-server era enabled by the birth of personal computers, to the Internet era where the enterprise was able to connect to the rest of the world through a network of computers that spanned the globe. Back in the mainframe days, systems were centrally controlled and managed. The mainframe administrators were the powerful gatekeepers of all data and all systems. They were also often the biggest bottleneck because nothing could get done without going through them. When the PC was born, IT professionals were empowered and were able to distribute workloads across many work nodes without having to go through the once-powerful mainframe gatekeepers. This was both advantageous and dangerous. It was advantageous from the standpoint that systems were built and deployed faster, cheaper, and with richer features. It was dangerous from the standpoint that in return for the gains in agility and flexibility, we witnessed a huge decrease in the effectiveness of governance and security.

Another way to say it is we gave up manageability and standardization for speed to market. The distributed nature of PCs in a client-server architecture created a "Wild West" effect, where applications could be deployed rapidly without the assurance of the proper security and controls in place. The net result was applications became more nonstandard and filled with gaping security holes that gave birth to the rise of security breaches, identity theft, and cyber-threats at levels never witnessed before.

In addition, management of the enterprise became a very complex and expensive challenge. In fact, one could argue that the birth of the client-server era was the defining moment where business and IT alignment took a turn for the worst. In the mainframe days, the mainframe and IT's sole purpose was to build systems for the business to enable business strategies. We built financial systems, payroll systems, and systems that drove the business's core competencies and automated operational processes. The PC-enabled client-server era allowed IT to create systems faster and cheaper but introduced new challenges like integration, interoperability, widespread patching, and much more. These complex issues led to a lot of IT-centric tasks that shifted large numbers of IT resources away from business enablement to IT maintenance. In addition, this era gave birth to a whole new breed of infrastructure, security, and operational professionals who spend the majority of their time working within IT silos dealing with issues and projects that do not drive revenue or increase profitability. In fact, much of this work increases opportunity costs for the business by consuming resources that could be directed toward increasing revenue or reducing waste.

Then came the Internet, which extended the enterprise to the outside world. Now companies could integrate their systems with their suppliers. Customers could go online and purchase goods and services in self-service mode 24 hours a day, 365 days a year. Software vendors could now deliver services as hosted solutions, eliminating the need to procure and manage hardware on-site. The Internet created a global revolution where any company or individual with an Internet connection could now do business from anywhere in the world, any hour of the day.

Once again, the level of complexity of systems increased dramatically. The level of control and governance decreased significantly. Applications became even more insecure, creating opportunities for people and organizations with bad intentions to attack systems and steal and sell data, which created a whole new industry of products and services to secure systems. When the Internet was being touted as a huge technology innovation, I remember the pundits fighting the movement while waving the security flag. This is the exact same thing we are witnessing today with the adoption of cloud computing. The same people and others like them are riding the security bandwagon in resistance to the next biggest thing in technology.

What history shows us time and time again is that every new technology innovation is met with resistance. Early adopters and risk takers embrace the new technologies and become the guinea pigs for the enterprises that typically prefer to wait until the technology becomes mature. The trailblazers take advantage of these new technologies and create tremendous business value. As success stories start becoming more and more frequent, demand goes up. As demand goes up, issues like standards and security become prominent topics and major hurdles for mass adoption. Standards start to emerge, best practices are published, and vendor and open-source products start becoming widely available to fill in the gaps. Cloud computing, like the Internet several years before, is at that tipping point where many organizations are moving from the *why* question to the *how* question.

In Figure 1.1, the diagram uses the Gartner Hype Cycle terminology to describe how technology matures over time.

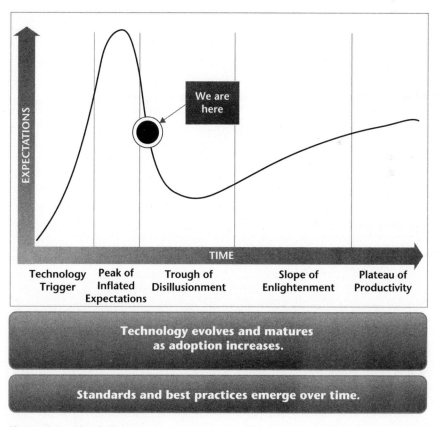

Figure 1.1 Cloud Maturity

As time progresses and more companies adopt cloud technology, the expectations move from hype and confusion in the early years and migrate toward broad acceptance as standards, best practices, and success stories emerge. Currently we are somewhere between the peak of inflated expectations and the disillusionment. As of this writing in early 2013, cloud computing is widely accepted by start-ups and small and medium businesses (SMBs), but large enterprises are late in adopting cloud computing. This is due to the complexities that come with years of legacy architectures, existing infrastructure and data centers, and organizational challenges.

The mind-set of large enterprises is changing rapidly in 2013 as many cloud service providers are delivering products and services that cater to enterprise-class clouds, where previously only commodity-class clouds were available. Commodity clouds were designed to commoditize infrastructure and offer it at low cost with the capabilities to achieve high scale and self-service capabilities. Enterprise-class clouds were designed to meet or exceed the security and service level agreements (SLAs) of the on-premises infrastructure they replace. Enterprise clouds are more expensive and complex than commodity clouds, but commodity clouds often do not meet the security, regulatory, and SLA requirements required within the enterprise.

Figure 1.2 shows how security maturity often lags behind in the adoption of new technologies, which delays mass adoption by large enterprises. The early pioneers and risk takers blaze the trail and eventually the best practices and security vendor solutions emerge from those early lessons learned. It appears that 2013 will be the year where enterprises start to embrace cloud computing in large numbers, as we are seeing huge turnouts to cloud computing conferences and a large increase in budget dollars allocated for cloud computing.

Enter the Cloud

Cloud computing combines the best of the mainframe era with the best of the PC-enabled client-server era along with the Internet era. Those old-timers from the conference I mentioned earlier were right. "We have been doing this for years," as they said. What they missed, though, is that now we can do it at scale, using a pay-as-you-go billing model, at speeds never accomplished before, and all without ever buying any hardware or building any data centers. If managed correctly, cloud computing can give us back a lot of that central control and governance that we had from the mainframe days. At the same time, the cloud makes available to us a massive amount of distributed computing resources, gives us broad network access over the Internet, and bottles it

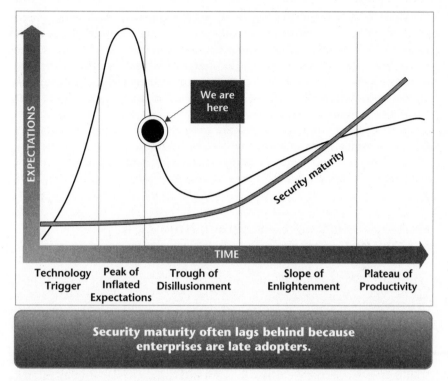

Figure 1.2   Cloud Security Maturity

up so we can pay for it as a utility like electricity or water. We pay for what we use and we turn it off when we don't need it.

It is true that many of the concepts of cloud computing have been around for years. What is new is that many of those lessons learned and techniques in computer science that have been perfected over the past few decades are now able to be simplified and automated and made available as highly abstracted on-demand services and offered at price points that are hard for the traditional on-premises or commercial software industry to compete against. The days of requiring customers to purchase and manage hardware and software licenses are long gone. Most customers now expect their needs to be met over the web either as an on-demand software solution (Software as a Service), a platform for quickly developing scalable solutions without all of the infrastructure costs (Platform as a Service), or a virtual data center for building scalable solutions at a lower cost (Infrastructure as a Service). These three cloud service models will be discussed in detail in Chapter 2.

When people tell me that the cloud is nothing new and that we have been doing cloud for years and years, I give them this analogy. "The iPhone is nothing new. We have been doing phones for years and years." My point here is, yes, we have been using telephones for decades and decades, but the iPhone is radically different from the rotary phone that I used as a kid, and it has made a major impact on businesses and on our lives. The cloud is to computing as the iPhone is to telephones.

Still not convinced? Here are some case studies of companies leveraging cloud computing to create business value. Each case study has a very compelling story of how great teams leveraged the cloud to get to market fast, scaled to incredible levels, and did it without buying hardware.

Start-Up Case Study: Instagram, from Zero to a Billion Overnight

In October 2010, a photo-sharing application called Instagram was launched, and 25,000 people registered on that first day. Three months later, Instagram had 1 million users, and shortly after hit 10 million. At that time, the company only offered an iOS version of its mobile application, so it was only capturing iPhone users. A year and a half later, Instagram had close to 30 million users. When it finally launched the Android version, it acquired 1 million users on the first day. In April 2012, less than two years after it launched, Instagram was bought by Facebook for an estimated $1 billion. In September 2012, just shy of two years from its initial launch, Instagram hit 100 million users.

Wow! Three guys on a bootstrap budget were able to build a solution entirely on a public cloud. Imagine trying to scale that fast in a brick-and-mortar data center. In a physical data center, they would never be able to buy hardware fast enough to keep up with the skyrocketing growth. In fact, one could argue that if it were not for the cloud and the on-demand and auto-scaling capabilities, they may never have been able to achieve this success because they would have likely experienced outages as they ran out of capacity.

This story highlights the power of on-demand compute resources. These talented engineers were able to build an amazing, highly scalable architecture in a short amount of time. They did not have to manage data centers or networks or procure, install, and manage hardware. Instead they focused on application architecture and the user experience, two things they excelled at. For start-ups, the cloud is a no-brainer. For companies with an existing data center, it is more of a challenge, which leads us to our next case study.

Established Company Case Study: Netflix, Shifting from On-Premises to the Cloud

Netflix is an industry leader in streaming video content over the Internet. In 2009, 100 percent of all customer traffic was run through Netflix's own data center. By the end of 2010, much of that same traffic was running on AWS, Amazon's public cloud solution. Netflix's goal for 2013 is to have at least 95 percent of all services, including operational services, not just customer traffic, running in the cloud. On its technology blog the company stated its reasons for shifting to the cloud. The enormous amount of incoming traffic required it to rearchitect its solution. It decided that it would rather focus its engineering efforts on building and improving the business applications (Netflix's core competencies) and let Amazon focus on the infrastructure (AWS's core competency). Netflix also spoke about how challenging it was to predict traffic. Companies building on-premises solutions must buy excess capacity to handle spikes. That becomes a great challenge when traffic is not predictable. Netflix felt it was advantageous to leverage the public cloud's on-demand resources and focus on building in auto-scaling capabilities to ensure that it could consume compute resources at the same rate of its incoming traffic. According to the Netflix technology blog on December 14, 2010:

> Cloud environments are ideal for horizontally scaling architectures. We don't have to guess months ahead what our hardware, storage, and networking needs are going to be. We can programmatically access more of these resources from shared pools within AWS almost instantly.

Netflix also sees leveraging cloud computing as a competitive advantage. The company is able to scale at amazing levels* while controlling costs and reducing the risks of downtime. It also feels that the cloud is the wave of the future and leveraging the cloud will attract the best talent:

> It will help foster a competitive environment for cloud service providers, which will help keep innovation high and prices dropping. We chose to be pioneers in this transition so we could leverage our investment as we grow, rather than to double down on a model we expect will decline in the industry. We think this will help differentiate Netflix as a place to work, and it will help us scale our business.

Now we have discussed a start-up success story and an established company success story in the cloud. Let's take a look at how the government is leveraging the cloud.

---

*As of November 2012, Netflix accounts for 29 percent of all Internet traffic in North America.

Government Case Study: NOAA, E-mail, and Collaboration in the Cloud

The National Oceanic and Atmospheric Administration (NOAA) moved to a cloud-based e-mail solution—Google's Gmail—at the beginning of 2012. NOAA is a federal agency with over 25,000 employees whose mission is to understand and predict change in climate, weather, oceans, and coasts. NOAA has employees working in all conditions such as in the air, on land, and on sea. The employees rely heavily on Internet-connected devices and collaboration with team members and other agencies. To enable efficient e-mail and collaboration capabilities, NOAA chose a cloud-based solution that includes e-mail, instant messaging, videoconferencing, shared calendars, and shared documents. Migrating to these cloud services cut NOAA's costs in half and removed the burden of managing software and hardware updates in a highly distributed and device-heavy environment. NOAA's management staff claims that the cloud-based e-mail and collaboration tools are faster and easier to deploy than the on-premises solutions and the services themselves were more modern. Moving its e-mail and collaboration services to the cloud created great business value by delivering a better overall service at half the price with less effort.

We have discussed success stories in the private sector and the public sector. The next case study is an amazing story about a presidential campaign that built a billion-dollar e-commerce site overnight.

Not-for-Profit Case Study: Obama Campaign, Six-Month Shelf-Life with One Big Peak

Very rarely does one see the type of requirements that the Obama campaign's technical team was faced with. They very quickly had to build a suite of applications including an e-commerce fund-raising platform capable of managing over $1 billion that would run for only six months, have an enormous spike on the last few days, and then back everything up and go away. The team relied heavily on cloud computing solutions and used services from every service model (SaaS, PaaS, and IaaS). The team cited reasons like lower costs, speed to market, on-demand resources, and scalability as some of the reasons for its decisions. Its phone-calling application scaled to 7,000 concurrent users as it peaked on Election Day. The team spent roughly $1.5 million on web hosting and web services, but the amazing statistic is that over $1 million of that was for an on-premises hosting company that managed some of the social media and digital advertising while the rest of the 200-plus applications ran on less than $500,000 of cloud infrastructure and services.

Summary

Cloud computing has evolved from many decades of computing. Cloud computing is the biggest technological shift since the birth of the personal computer and
the broad adoption of the Internet. Cloud computing is still in its infancy. Early
adopters were mainly start-ups, small businesses, and risk-taking enterprises. As
2012 closed out and the year 2013 began, cloud computing has become widely
accepted and enterprise budgets for cloud computing initiatives are growing at
enormous rates. As with anything new and immature, cloud computing is still
lacking in standards and best practices. The cloud vendors have occasional outages but their overall performance has improved over the years as their products
and services mature. Incredible success stories like Netflix and Instagram are
becoming more common each year. Enterprises are shifting dollars away from
commercial software licenses and hardware investments in favor of a variety of
cloud services across all three service models. The secret to success for enterprises will be picking the right cloud solutions to solve the right business problems. Understanding the three cloud service models—SaaS, PaaS, and IaaS—is
crucial for enterprises to make the right investments in the cloud.

References

Barr, J. (2012, November 16). "AWS in Action: Behind the Scenes of a Presidential Campaign." Retrieved from http://aws.typepad.com/aws/2012/11/aws-in-
action-behind-the-scenes-of-a-presidential-campaign.html.

Barton, M. (2012, April 11). "Cloud Lessons? Instagram Keep-It-Simple Mashup
Approach." Retrieved from http://www.wired.com/insights/2012/04/instagram/.

Ciancutti, J. (2010, December 14). "Four Reasons We Choose Amazon's Cloud as Our
Cloud Computing Platform." Retrieved from http://techblog.netflix.com/2010/12/
four-reasons-we-choose-amazons-cloud-as.html.

Cutler, K. (2012, April 9). "From 0 to $1B in Two Years: Instagram's Rose-Tinted Ride to Glory."
Retrieved from http://techcrunch.com/2012/04/09/instagram-story-facebook-acquisition/.

Fingas, J. (2012, November 8). "Sandvine: Netflix up to 29 Percent of North
American Internet Traffic, YouTube Is Fast on the Rise." Retrieved from
http://www.engadget.com/2012/11/08/sandvine-netflix-29-percent-of-north-
american-internet-traffic/.

Gallagher, S. (2012, November 20). "How Team Obama's Tech Efficiency Left Romney IT
in Dust." Retrieved from http://arstechnica.com/information-technology/2012/11/
how-team-obamas-tech-efficiency-left-romney-it-in-dust/.

Hoover, J. (2011, June 9). "From Ocean to Cloud: NOAA Goes Google Apps." Retrieved
from http://www.informationweek.com/government/cloud-saas/from-ocean-to-cloud-
noaa-goes-google-app/230500174.

Rush, K. (2012, November 12). "Meet the Obama Campaign's $250 Million Fundraising
Platform." Retrieved from http://kylerush.net/blog/meet-the-obama-campaigns-250-
million-fundraising-platform/.

Thibodeau, P. (2012, September 11). "Netflix Guts Data Center in Shift to Cloud." Retrieved
from   http://www.computerworld.com/s/article/9231146/Netflix_guts_data_center_
in_shift_to_cloud.

CHAPTER 2

Cloud Service Models

This is what our customers are asking for to take them to the next level and free them from the bondage of mainframe and client-server software.

—Marc Benioff, CEO, Salesforce.com

Choosing the right service model is a critical success factor for delivering cloud-based solutions. In order to choose the right service model or combination of service models, one must fully understand what each service model is and what responsibilities the cloud service providers assume versus the responsibilities the cloud service consumer assumes.

Infrastructure as a Service

There are three cloud service models: Software as a Service (SaaS), Platform as a Service (PaaS), and Infrastructure as a Service (IaaS). Each cloud service model provides a level of abstraction that reduces the efforts required by the service consumer to build and deploy systems. In a traditional on-premises data center, the IT team has to build and manage everything. Whether the team is building proprietary solutions from scratch or purchasing commercial software products, they have to install and manage one-to-many servers, develop and install the software, ensure that the proper levels of security are applied, apply patches routinely (operating system, firmware, application, database, and so on), and much more. Each cloud service model provides levels of abstraction and automation for these tasks, thus providing more agility to the cloud service consumers so they can focus more time on their business problems and less time on managing infrastructure.

Figure 2.1 displays what is called the *cloud stack*. At the bottom is the traditional data center, which may have some virtualization in place but does not have any of the characteristics of cloud computing.*

---

*The five characteristics of cloud computing are network access, elasticity, resource pooling, measured service, and on-demand self-service.

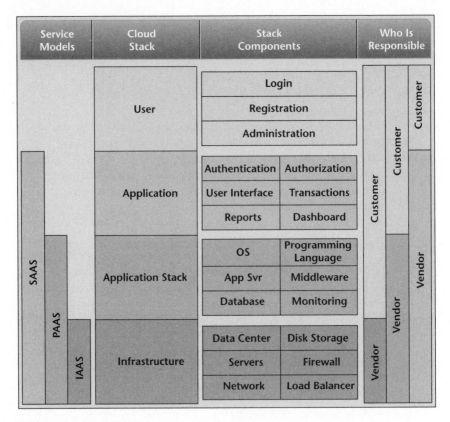

Figure 2.1   Cloud Stack

The next level up is IaaS. The National Institute of Standards and Technology (NIST) defines IaaS as:

> The capability provided to the consumer is to provision processing, storage, networks, and other fundamental computing resources where the consumer is able to deploy and run arbitrary software, which can include operating systems and applications. The consumer does not manage or control the underlying cloud infrastructure but has control over operating systems, storage, and deployed applications and possibly limited control of select networking components (e.g., host firewalls).

The Cloud Security Alliance (CSA), a standards organization for cloud security, states that IaaS:

> Delivers computer infrastructure (typically a platform virtualization environment) as a service, along with raw storage and networking.

Rather than purchasing servers, software, data center space, or network equipment, clients instead buy those resources as a fully outsourced service.

With IaaS, many of the tasks related to managing and maintaining a physical data center and physical infrastructure (servers, disk storage, networking, and so forth) are abstracted and available as a collection of services that can be accessed and automated from code- and/or web-based management consoles. Developers still have to design and code entire applications and administrators still need to install, manage, and patch third-party solutions, but there is no physical infrastructure to manage anymore. Gone are the long procurement cycles where people would order physical hardware from vendors that would ship the hardware to the buyer who then had to unpackage, assemble, and install the hardware, which consumed space within a data center. With IaaS, the virtual infrastructure is available on demand and can be up and running in minutes by calling an application programming interface (API) or launching from a web-based management console. Like utilities such as electricity or water, virtual infrastructure is a metered service that costs money when it is powered on and in use, but stops accumulating costs when it is turned off. In summary, IaaS provides virtual data center capabilities so service consumers can focus more on building and managing applications and less on managing data centers and infrastructure.

There are several IaaS vendors in the marketplace and too many to name in this book. The most mature and widely used IaaS cloud service provider is Amazon Web Services (AWS). Rackspace and GoGrid are also early pioneers in this space. OpenStack is an open source project that provides IaaS capabilities for those consumers who want to avoid vendor lock-in and want the control to build their own IaaS capabilities in-house, which is referred to as a *private cloud*. There are a number of companies that are building IaaS solutions on top of OpenStack similar to how there are many different distributions of Linux.

Platform as a Service

The next level up on the stack is PaaS. What IaaS is to infrastructure, PaaS is to the applications. PaaS sits on top of IaaS and abstracts much of the standard application stack–level functions and provides those functions as a service. For example, developers designing high-scaling systems often have to write a large amount of code to handle caching, asynchronous messaging, database scaling, and much more. Many PaaS solutions provide those capabilities as a service so the developers can focus on business logic and not reinvent the wheel by coding for underlying IT "plumbing." NIST defines PaaS as:

> The capability provided to the consumer is to deploy onto the cloud infrastructure consumer-created or acquired applications created using programming languages, libraries, services, and tools supported by the provider. The consumer does not manage or control the underlying cloud infrastructure, including network, servers, operating systems, or storage, but has control over the deployed applications and possibly configuration settings for the application-hosting environment.

The CSA describes PaaS as:

> The delivery of a computing platform and solution stack as a service. PaaS offerings facilitate deployment of applications without the cost and complexity of buying and managing the underlying hardware and software and provisioning hosting capabilities.

The CSA also mentions that PaaS services are available entirely from the Internet. PaaS vendors manage the application platform and provide the developers with a suite of tools to expedite the development process. Developers give up a degree of flexibility with PaaS because they are constrained by the tools and the software stacks that the PaaS vendor offers. The developers also have little-to-no control over lower-level software controls like memory allocation and stack configurations (examples: number of threads, amount of cache, patch levels, etc.).

The PaaS vendors control all of that and may even throttle how much compute power a service consumer can use so that the vendor can ensure the platform scales equally for everyone. Chapter 5 ("Choosing the Right Cloud Service Model") explores these service model characteristics in great detail. Early PaaS pioneers like Force.com, Google Apps Engine, and Microsoft Azure dictated both the platform stack and the underlying infrastructure to developers. Force.com dictates that developers write in Apex code and the underlying infrastructure must be on Force.com's data center. Google Apps Engine originally required that developers code in Python and on the Google data center while Azure originally required .NET technologies on Microsoft data centers. A new breed of PaaS vendors have emerged and have created an open PaaS environment where consumers can implement the PaaS platform on the infrastructure of their choice and with many options for the development stack, including PHP, Ruby, Python, Node.js, and others. This approach is critical for widespread adoption by enterprises since many enterprises require or prefer to keep some or all of the application on-premises in a private cloud. Often, large enterprises leverage hybrid clouds by keeping their data in a private cloud and moving non-mission-critical components into the public cloud.* Both Google and Microsoft now support multiple development languages, whereas in the past they only supported one.

Heroku and Engine Yard are examples of mature public PaaS solutions that provide multiple stacks for developers, although at the time of the writing of this book they can be deployed only on AWS. Another huge advantage of PaaS is that these platforms integrate with numerous third-party software solutions, which are often referred to as plugins, add-ons, or extensions. Here are some examples of categories of extensions that can be found in most mature PaaS solutions:

- Database
- Logging
- Monitoring
- Security
- Caching
- Search
- E-mail
- Analytics
- Payments

By leveraging APIs to access numerous third-party solutions, developers can provide fail over, high service level agreements (SLAs), and achieve huge gains in speed to market and cost efficiency since they don't have to manage and maintain the technology behind the APIs. This is the power of PaaS, where developers can quickly assemble a collection of mature and proven third-party solutions simply by calling APIs and not having to go through a procurement process followed by an implementation process for each third-party tool. PaaS allows companies to focus on their core competencies and integrate with the best-of-breed tools in the marketplace. PaaS is the least mature of the three cloud service models but analysts predict a huge boom in the PaaS marketplace in the next several years.[†]

Software as a Service

At the top of the stack is SaaS. SaaS is a complete application delivered as a service to the service consumer. The service consumer has only to configure

---

*A private cloud is an IaaS or PaaS deployed within a service consumer's own datacenter or hosting facility's data center and is not deployed on a shared grid with other customers. Public cloud is an IaaS or PaaS that is running on another company's data center in a shared environment with other customers.
[†]Gartner predicts PaaS revenues near $1.5 billion in 2013, compared to $900 million in 2011.

some application-specific parameters and manage users. The service provider handles all of the infrastructure, all of the application logic, all deployments, and everything pertaining to the delivery of the product or service. Some very common SaaS applications are customer relationship management (CRM), enterprise resource planning (ERP), payroll, accounting, and other common business software. SaaS solutions are extremely common for non-core-competency functionality. Companies choose to rely on SaaS solutions for non-core functions so they do not have to support the application infrastructure, provide maintenance, and hire staff to manage it all. Instead they pay a subscription fee and simply use the service over the Internet as a browser-based service. NIST defines SaaS as:

> The capability provided to the consumer is to use the provider's applications running on a cloud infrastructure. The applications are accessible from various client devices through either a thin client interface, such as a web browser (e.g., web-based email), or a program interface. The consumer does not manage or control the underlying cloud infrastructure, including network, servers, operating systems, storage, or even individual application capabilities, with the possible exception of limited user-specific application configuration settings.

Deployment Models

Even though the focus of this book is on cloud service models, it is important to understand the deployment models of cloud computing as well. Figure 2.2 shows the NIST visual model of cloud computing.

The NIST definition of a public cloud states:

> The cloud infrastructure is provisioned for open use by the general public. It may be owned, managed, and operated by a business, academic, or government organization, or some combination of them. It exists on the premises of the cloud provider.

A public cloud is a multitenant environment where the end user pays for usage of resources on a shared grid of commodity resources alongside other customers. The end users have no visibility into the physical location of where their software is running other than where the data center is located. An abstraction layer is built on top of the physical hardware and exposed as APIs to the end user, who leverages these APIs to create virtual compute resources that run in a large pool of resources shared by many. Here are some advantages of public clouds:

- **Utility pricing.** The end user pays only for the resources it consumes. This allows the end user to turn on more cloud services when it needs

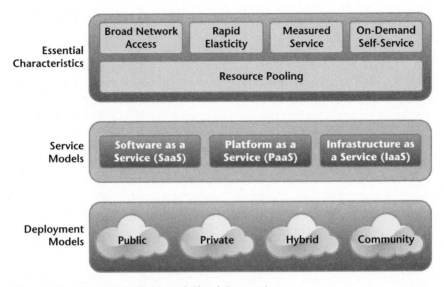

Figure 2.2   The NIST Definition of Cloud Computing

to scale up and turn off cloud services when it needs to scale down. The end user no longer needs to procure physical hardware in this model and therefore has a huge opportunity to eliminate wasted compute cycles by consuming only what is needed, when it is needed.

- **Elasticity**. The end user has a seemingly endless pool of resources at its disposal and can configure its software solutions to dynamically increase or decrease the amount of compute resources it needs to handle peak loads. This allows the end user to react in real time to abnormal spikes in traffic, where in a private on-premises cloud or a noncloud solution the end user would have to already own or lease the necessary resources in order to handle peaks.

- **Core competency**. By leveraging public clouds, the end user is essentially outsourcing its data center and infrastructure management to companies whose core competency is managing infrastructure. In return, the end user spends less time managing infrastructure and more time focusing on its own core competency.

Public clouds have some huge benefits but they also have drawbacks. Here is a list of some of the risks of leveraging a public cloud.

- **Control**. End users must rely on the public cloud vendor to meet their SLAs for performance and uptime. If a public cloud provider has an outage and the end user has not architected properly for redundancy, it is at the mercy of the cloud vendor to restore services.

- **Regulatory issues**. Regulations like PCI DSS (Payment Card Industry Data Security Standard), HIPAA (Health Information Portability and Accountability Act), and data privacy issues can make it challenging to deploy in a public cloud. It often requires a hybrid solution to meet these regulations, although we are starting to see some companies solve these issues entirely in the public cloud by leveraging certified SaaS solutions for those components that are hard to audit in a public cloud.
- **Limited configurations**. Public cloud vendors have a standard set of infrastructure configurations that meet the needs of the general public. Sometimes very specific hardware is required to solve intensive computational problems. In cases like this the public cloud is often not an option because the required infrastructure is simply not offered by the vendor.

A private cloud is defined as:

The cloud infrastructure is provisioned for exclusive use by a single organization comprising multiple consumers (e.g., business units). It may be owned, managed, and operated by the organization, a third party, or some combination of them, and it may exist on or off premises.

The advantage of a private cloud is that it addresses the disadvantages of the public cloud defined earlier (control, regulatory issues, and configurations). Private clouds can be on-premises or hosted in a cloud provider's data center. In either case, private cloud end users deploy on a single-tenant environment and are not comingled with other customers. For on-premises private cloud implementations, cloud service consumers are in control of their own destiny since they still manage the data center and they have the flexibility of procuring any hardware configuration they desire. Hosted private cloud users are still dependent on their cloud service provider to provide infrastructure, but their resources are not shared with other customers. This offers the user more control and security but costs more than leveraging compute resources in a multitenant public cloud. Private clouds reduce some of the regulatory risks around data ownership, privacy, and security due to the single-tenant nature of the deployment model.

However, leveraging private clouds sacrifices some of the core advantages of cloud computing, namely rapid elasticity, resource pooling, and pay-as-you-go pricing. Private clouds do allow end users to scale up and down over a shared pool of resources, but those resources are limited to the amount of infrastructure that is bought and managed internally as opposed to leveraging a seemingly endless grid of compute resources that are readily available. This drives up costs and reduces agility because internal resources have to manage all of this physical infrastructure, and excess capacity must be procured and managed. Having excess capacity also destroys the pay-as-you-go model because the end user has already paid for the infrastructure whether it uses it or not.

To get the best of both worlds, many organizations leverage both public and private clouds, which is called a *hybrid cloud*. A hybrid cloud is defined as:

> A composition of two or more distinct cloud infrastructures (private, community, or public) that remain unique entities, but are bound together by standardized or proprietary technology that enables data and application portability (e.g., cloud bursting for load balancing between clouds).

A best practice for hybrid clouds is to use the public cloud as much as possible to get all the benefits of cloud computing like rapid elasticity and resource pooling, but leverage the private cloud where the risks in areas of data ownership and privacy are too high for the public cloud.

AEA CASE STUDY: Choosing Cloud Service Models

Our fictitious company mentioned in the preface, Acme eAuctions (AEA), built its entire infrastructure on-premises before cloud computing was a marketing buzzword. AEA's management believes that moving to the cloud can give the company a competitive advantage in the following areas:

- Speed to market
- Flexibility
- Scalability
- Cost

AEA already has a huge investment in physical infrastructure, so its shift to the cloud will have to occur one piece of infrastructure and one application domain at a time. Since AEA already has a mature data center, it may choose to keep certain pieces of its architecture on-premises in a private cloud (for example, payment processing) and others in the public cloud. AEA is a prime candidate for leveraging a hybrid cloud solution. If AEA were a start-up and building a solution from scratch, it would likely build its solution 100 percent in the public cloud to eliminate the need to raise capital for building or leasing multiple data centers. For parts of its application, such as payment processing, that it deems too critical to put in a public cloud, it could leverage a SaaS solution that is certified for regulatory controls, such as PCI DSS.

The point here is that there is no one right answer to any problem. Companies have many options when it comes to cloud computing, which is why it is critical that management, architects, product managers, and developers understand the different deployment models as well as the service models. We will discuss these key decision points with more AEA examples in Chapter 5 ("Choosing the Right Cloud Service Model").

Summary

Cloud computing is revolutionizing the way software is built and delivered. We are in a paradigm shift, moving away from a legacy model where we buy and control infrastructure and build or buy software to a new world where we consume everything as services. It is critical that managers and architects fully understand the pros and cons of cloud computing, the definitions of each cloud service model, and the definitions of each cloud deployment model. When leveraged properly, cloud computing can bring an organization unprecedented agility and greatly reduced costs while connecting the organization to a global collection of services. However, if cloud computing is not fully understood, an organization can find itself building yet another collection of IT-silo-based software solutions that never delivers on its promises to the business.

References

Gartner. (2012, November 19). "Gartner Says Worldwide Platform as a Service Revenue Is on Pace to Reach $1.2B." Press Release. Retrieved from http://www.gartner.com/it/page.jsp?id=2242415.

Mell, P., and T. Grance (2011, September). "The NIST Definition of Cloud Computing: Recommendations of the National Institute of Standards and Technology." Retrieved from http://csrc.nist.gov/publications/nistpubs/800–145/SP800–145.pdf.

Security Guidance for Critical Areas of Focus in Cloud Computing v3.0. (2011). Retrieved from https://cloudsecurityalliance.org/guidance/csaguide.v3.0.pdf.

CHAPTER 3

Cloud Computing Worst Practices

When you come to a fork in the road, take it.
—YOGI BERRA, HALL OF FAME BASEBALL PLAYER

The U.S. Army invested $2.7 billion in a cutting-edge cloud-based solution with the goal of communicating real-time information from various sources to assist in battlefield operations in Iraq and Afghanistan. The system failed to deliver and actually hindered operations instead of helping. As one person put it, "Almost any commercial software product out there would be better." Cloud computing can create huge competitive advantages if applications and services are correctly architected to satisfy the business requirements. This chapter discusses the nine common mistakes that companies make in the cloud. At the end of the discussion for each common mistake, recommendations for avoiding these mistakes are given.

Avoiding Failure When Moving to the Cloud

Historically, many companies fail when it comes to implementing new and transformational technologies. There are many causes of failure. Sometimes companies fail because they don't fully understand or embrace new technologies. Sometimes they rush into development mode and forgo the necessary architecture and design steps. Sometimes they have unrealistic expectations like too-aggressive due dates, too large of a scope, not the right people, and many other reasons. The next few sections focus on the top reasons why companies moving to the cloud might fail.

Migrating Applications to the Cloud

A common misperception about cloud computing is the notion that migrating existing applications to the cloud is a simple solution that drives down costs. The reality is usually the complete opposite. In fact, very few applications are good candidates to move to the cloud in their current architecture. Legacy software is architected to run within the corporate firewalls of the company. If the software was built several years ago, there is a high probability that the software is highly dependent on the physical hardware it runs on and possibly even on the technology stack it was written on. This is often referred to as being a *tightly coupled* architecture, because the software cannot function properly if it is separated from its physical environment. Cloud computing architectures require a *loosely coupled* architecture. As mentioned in Chapter 2, elasticity is a key component of cloud computing. For software to be truly elastic, meaning it is able to be scaled up and down as needed, it must be independent of its physical environment.

Most legacy architectures were never intended to be built in a manner where the system automatically scales as the number of transactions increases. Traditional scaling techniques often rely solely on vertical scaling. Vertical scaling is accomplished by increasing the existing hardware either by adding more CPUs, memory, or disk space to the existing infrastructure or by replacing the existing infrastructure with bigger and more powerful hardware. Vertical scaling is known as *scaling up*. Vertical scaling typically does not require software changes beyond changing configurations to allow the software to leverage the new infrastructure as long as the same type of infrastructure is used.

With this type of scaling strategy, architects often forgo designing their software to be independent of the infrastructure. For example, if an application is built on an IBM iSeries computer, the software is typically written in ways to take full advantage of the proprietary infrastructure, thus becoming tightly coupled to the hardware. Migrating an application like that would take a major reengineering to remove the dependencies from the iSeries so that the application can become elastic in the cloud. For a system to be elastic it must be able to handle unanticipated and sudden spikes in workloads.

If elasticity is not the reason for moving the application to the cloud and the company just does not want to manage and maintain the infrastructure anymore, then what the company most likely needs is a hosting solution. Hosting is not the same thing as cloud computing. Hosting does not provide for the five characteristics of cloud computing: broad network access, elasticity, measured service, on-demand self-service, and resource pooling. Hosting is simply renting or buying infrastructure and floor space at a hosting provider's facility. Think of migrating to a hosting facility as forklifting an application from site A to site B. Migrating an application to the cloud is much more involved than that.

Scaling in the cloud can be done with vertical scaling but is mostly accomplished through automated horizontal scaling. Horizontal scaling is accomplished by adding additional infrastructure that runs in conjunction with the existing infrastructure. This is known as *scaling out*.

Horizontal scaling is often done at multiple layers of the architecture. Some common horizontal scaling methods are to add nodes by server farm type (Figure 3.1), by customer type, and by application domain type (Figure 3.2).

Scaling at the Product Level

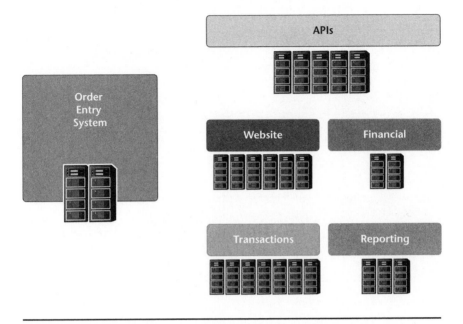

Scaling at the Technology Component Level

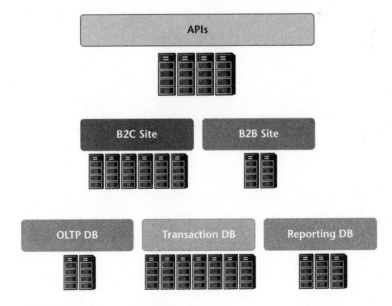

Figure 3.1   Scale by Server Farm Type

Uptime and Scalability Strategies

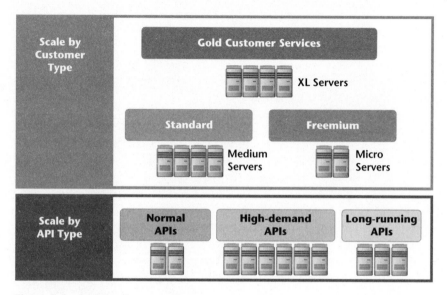

Figure 3.2   Scale by Customer Type

We will discuss these design patterns in detail in Chapter 4 ("It Starts with Architecture").

Another challenge for legacy applications is whether the system design is stateful or stateless. Cloud services are stateless. A *stateless* service is a service that is unaware of any information from previous requests or responses and is only aware of information during the duration of the time that the service is processing a given request. Stateless services store the application state on the client, not the server, and therefore do not have a dependency on the infrastructure. For example, if a loan service receives a request to evaluate the credit rating of a customer applying for a loan, the service has no record of any information about the customer until it receives an incoming message (usually as an XML or JSON document). After it processes the document, determines the credit score, and responds back to the requestor, it does not store any of the information within the session and no longer knows anything about the customer.

We will discuss application state in more detail in Chapter 6 ("The Key to the Cloud") to explain why stateless architectures are better suited for the cloud than stateful architectures. The work required to change the underlying architecture from maintaining state to being stateless is often not feasible and a total replacement of the application is a more realistic approach. Companies that migrate legacy stateful applications to the cloud will likely be disappointed with the end result if they expect to reap all of the benefits of cloud computing.

In summary, unless an on-premises application was architected as a collection of loosely coupled services to be accessed by other technology and infrastructure-agnostic services, then migrating to the cloud either will take a major reengineering effort, will not reap many of the benefits of the cloud, or might be completely unfeasible.

Recommendation: First, make sure the architects have a keen understanding of the differences between stateless and stateful design patterns. Understand if an application is a good candidate for migrating to the cloud or if hosting or a rewrite is a better option.

Misguided Expectations

Another common mistake is that companies often take on cloud computing initiatives with inflated expectations. There are many impressive success stories in recent years as companies large and small have embraced the cloud. On April 9, 2012, Facebook CEO Mark Zuckerberg posted on Facebook that his company had just purchased start-up Instagram for its innovative mobile photo-sharing platform for $1 billion. At the time it was purchased, the entire company consisted of only 13 people and had over 100 servers running in the Amazon cloud supporting over 30 million users. In its first year of existence with only 3 engineers, the platform went from 0 to 14 million users with over 150 million photos and several terabytes of traffic.

Another star of the cloud is Netflix. By late 2012, Netflix laid claim to the fact that almost 29 percent of all Internet traffic flowed through its streaming video platform to televisions, computers, and devices to consumers in North America, bypassing YouTube and even HTTP. The team at Netflix is a poster child for how to run an innovative culture that pushes the envelope and uses the cloud as a competitive advantage.

Both Instagram and Netflix are outliers. Instagram had the luxury of starting from scratch and architecting for the cloud out of the gate. Netflix made a business decision to put all of its chips in the cloud and hired and trained an incredible engineering team who continue to be pioneers in cloud computing. Neither company represents a normal Fortune 500 company or an established small or medium-size business looking to leverage cloud services. Many organizations have a very complex enterprise consisting of numerous vendor and proprietary solutions ranging from mainframe technologies, to midsize computers, n-tier architectures, and every other architectural pattern that was popular at one time or another. Starting with a blank slate or getting an initiative from the CEO to re-platform the entire product line with a new cloud-based architecture is not the norm for most companies. Often management, or even the architects, are so starstruck by the success of companies like Netflix and Instagram that they expect similar results, an outcome they most likely can't achieve even if they do a good job architecting. Setting an expectation for the outcomes for a cloud computing initiative should be based on the business case in support of the initiative, not what other companies have achieved. Cloud computing is only part of the success these companies had. A bigger part of their success was their vision, the talent within their team, and their ability to execute.

One of the biggest misguided perceptions of cloud computing is that cloud initiatives will greatly reduce the cost of doing business. That may be true for some initiatives but not all of them; after all, cost is not the only reason to leverage the cloud. Even if a company has a good business case for reducing costs in the cloud, it takes more than cloud computing to achieve the cost reduction. Companies need to design with cost in mind. The cloud can be cost-effective if the architecture effectively optimizes its usage of cloud services. In order to optimize costs, the architecture must monitor the usage of cloud services and track costs.

Cloud services are a metered service where the cost is calculated on a pay-as-you-go model much like utilities such as electricity and water are in our homes. In legacy on-premises data centers, purchased infrastructure becomes a sunk cost, which depreciates on the books over the course of the several years. To plan for surges in traffic and growth over time, a company must overbuy so that there is excess capacity and usually redundancy for fail over at another location. These monies are paid in advance and much of this infrastructure may sit idle most of the time. A correctly architected cloud-based equivalent solution would allow a system to scale up and down as needed to align costs with revenues, the infamous pay-as-you-go-model. The key word there is *correctly* architected. If there are flaws in the architecture and the cloud services consumed are not appropriately turned off when not needed, the cloud can become a very expensive proposition. On the flipside, if the architecture does not scale up sufficiently or does not design for failure, the end result can be outages and poor performance, resulting in lost customers and revenue.

Not every problem is one that needs to be solved by cloud computing. For example, I once had a client call me and ask what cloud provider he should move his server to. When I asked him what problem he was trying to solve he said he had a code repository on a single server and wished to migrate it to the cloud. The asset cost him about $3,000 in hardware and software plus annual maintenance (if he was even paying for it). If he moved the server to the cloud at a 50-cents-an-hour rate, he would pay that rate every hour from this point forward. At 50 cents an hour, the server would cost $12 a day and for the year it would cost $4,380. To make matters worse, he would continue to pay that each year where his on-premises sunk cost of $3,000 was a one-time cost. Since his application did not need to scale up and down, was already paid for, and was not causing any issues, there was no business case for it to move to the cloud and it certainly was not going to be cheaper in the cloud. I proposed two solutions to him. Solution 1: Do nothing. Solution 2: Replace the on-premises solution with a Software as a Service (SaaS) equivalent solution. There are many SaaS-based code repositories that charge a minimal amount of money per month and do not require any hardware or software to manage.

Recommendation: Set realistic expectations. Break cloud computing initiatives into smaller deliverables in order to deliver business value sooner and allow the team to learn along the way. Do not try the big-bang approach where the team goes away for several months or a year with the hope of delivering a large number of new cloud services. Understand the pros and cons of each cloud service model. Design to optimize, monitor, and audit cloud service consumption and implement a governance process to enforce proper consumption patterns. Each monthly bill from cloud service providers should be closely monitored to ensure costs are within expectations.

Misinformed about Cloud Security

Security is another area where expectations are often off base and there are two camps. The first camp believes in the myths that cloud computing is catastrophically insecure and data cannot be placed in a public cloud for any reason. People in this camp refuse to consider public clouds and often resort to building their own private clouds. If security and infrastructure are not a core competency, then building private clouds based out of fear might not be the best use of company money and time. The second camp is the group that believes that security is taken care of for them by the cloud vendors. This camp then proceeds to deploy software and services with gaping security holes into the cloud, where cyber-criminals welcome them in with open arms.

The cloud is not only an enabler for enterprises but it is a great enabler for cyber-criminals as well for two reasons. First, cloud computing is still very immature and lacking standards at this time. There are not a lot of engineers with years of hands-on experience securing applications in the cloud. The end result is that many cloud services are being deployed by today's corporations without the necessary security and controls and are very vulnerable to all kinds of attacks and breaches. The second reason why the cloud is an enabler for cyber-criminals is that the cloud vendors are a huge target because they house compute resources and data for a large number of companies. The cloud providers typically provide high levels of perimeter security, but it is up to the companies deploying their services to build the appropriate level of application security. For example, an Infrastructure as a Service (IaaS) cloud provider like Amazon Web Services (AWS) has world-class secure data centers, white papers on how to build highly secure services on its platform, and provides a suite of application programming interfaces (APIs), making it easier to design for security. However, it is up to the architects building the software on AWS to encrypt the data, manage the keys, implement good password policies, and so forth.

The truth about security and the cloud is quite simple. With the proper security architecture, the public cloud *can be* more secure than most on-premises data centers. Unfortunately, very few corporations know enough about the security requirements in the cloud necessary to architect for it, and many others do not have skill sets internally to build the appropriate level of security. A recent report on security breaches from Forrester declares that 75 percent of all security breaches are inside jobs. Of the inside jobs 63 percent were not caused by intent. Examples of causes are lost, stolen, or misplaced assets such as thumb drives, disks, documents, devices, laptops, and so forth. Architects should sort through all the myths and hype about cloud security and research factual information.

Security is not something one buys; security must be planned and designed into software. Many of the security best practices that have been applied in data centers for years should be applied within the cloud, as well. We will discuss how to design for security in Chapter 9 ("Security Design in the Cloud"). What is important to note here is that deploying or leveraging cloud services requires additional steps to provide the appropriate level of security necessary to comply with regulatory constraints and to pass audits such as HIPAA, SOC-2, PCI DSS, and others. With the proper investment in infrastructure and application security, cloud services can be more secure than on-premises solutions, especially in organizations whose competency is not security.

Most non-Fortune 500 companies simply do not have the staff, expertise, and budget to build and maintain the appropriate levels of security to keep up with the increasing number of threats. For most cloud providers, security is a core competency and they invest heavily in talent and budget dollars to produce best-of-breed security solutions. Leveraging security as a service from a cloud computing vendor that excels at security can allow companies to obtain higher levels of security than they have achieved in the past in their own data centers. The trick is knowing what the security risks are and addressing those risks with a combination of technology, process, and governance.

Recommendation: Start by making sure the architects, the product team, and the security professionals have a broad understanding of cloud security, regulatory controls, and auditing requirements, which we will cover in detail in Chapter 9. If necessary, bring in an independent third party to perform an assessment and to perform audits prior to deployment and ongoing after deployment. Design for security up front. Do not try to plug the holes later.

Selecting a Favorite Vendor, Not an Appropriate Vendor

A common mistake many companies make is they don't thoroughly evaluate the cloud vendors and simply select vendors that they are familiar with. For an obvious example of this worst practice go to any .NET shop and the odds that it has selected Microsoft Azure are incredibly high. That is not to say that Azure is not a good technology, but it may not be the right tool for the job. In Chapter 5 ("Choosing the Right Cloud Service Model") we will discuss the business use cases that make sense for each service model. Azure is a Platform as a Service (PaaS). The fact that a company writes .NET code should not override the technical requirements that determine whether the best cloud service model is SaaS, PaaS, or IaaS. In fact, there are several PaaS solutions that support .NET development.

The same applies to Google App Engine. Google's PaaS supports Python development. Instagram is a Python shop. Had it defaulted to Google's PaaS due to its choice of Python as its stack, it might not have been able to achieve the scalability that it achieved on AWS. This by no means is a knock on Google or a declaration that AWS is any better than Google. Simply put, for scaling requirements like Instagram's, an IaaS provider is a better choice than a PaaS. PaaS providers have thresholds that they enforce within the layers of their architecture to ensure that one customer does not consume so many resources that it impacts the overall platform, resulting in performance degradation for other customers. With IaaS, there are fewer limitations, and much higher levels of scalability can be achieved with the proper architecture. We will revisit this use case in Chapter 5. Architects must not let their loyalty to their favorite vendor get in the way of making the best possible business decision. A hammer may be the favorite tool of a home builder, but when he needs to turn screws he should use a screwdriver.

Recommendation: Understand the differences between the three cloud service models: SaaS, PaaS, and IaaS. Know what business cases are best suited for each service model. Don't choose cloud vendors based solely on the software stack that the developers use or based on the vendor that the company has been buying hardware from for years.

Outages and Out-of-Business Scenarios

When leveraging cloud services there should be an expectation that everything can and will fail. It doesn't matter which cloud service model a company is relying on; everything fails at some point. It is no different from the power that runs our houses. All houses will encounter a power outage at some point, whether it is a brief flicker or an outage that lasts for hours or days. The same applies to cloud computing. A best practice is to design for failure. In Chapter 13 ("Disaster Recovery Planning") we will discuss best practices for dealing with failures for each service model. Here are a couple of examples where companies did not plan for failure.

PaaS provider Coghead was an early market mover in the database-as-a-service space. Database-as-a-service products create huge speed-to-market advantages through the automation of database administration tasks and by providing autoscaling capabilities. Customers leverage these services that allow them to focus more on their applications and less on database management, thus providing greater agility. Customers that leverage this type of service must understand that they are signing up for vendor lock-in and giving up some levels of control. Lock-in is nothing new in the world of databases. Companies have been buying Oracle, SQL Server, and DB2 licenses for decades and are used to being locked into a vendor. The difference with on-premises computing is that if the vendor goes away, the company still can use the software for as long as it wants. In the cloud, when the vendor goes away, the service often goes with it. In 2009, SAP purchased Coghead and gave customers eight weeks to get rid of their dependencies on Coghead because it was shutting down the service. Many customers never considered this scenario and were sent scrambling for the next eight weeks or more to recover from the shutdown of their database technology. A best practice for companies leveraging SaaS or PaaS database technologies is to ensure that they have access to the data outside of the service provider, whether it is snapshots of database backups, a daily extract, or some method of storing recoverable data independent of the service and the provider.

By now, everyone has seen the issues created by outages from major IaaS and PaaS providers like AWS, Rackspace, Microsoft, and Google. Even companies like Netflix, which has built a service called the Chaos Monkey, whose job is to break things in production to test real-time recovery of the overall platform, is not immune to outages.

When a provider like AWS has a service outage within one of its availability zones, a large number of its customers' websites and services go offline until AWS resolves the issue. Most of these customer outages could have been easily avoided had the customer anticipated and designed for failure. Many customers only deploy to a single zone and have no plan for recovery when that zone is impacted. A provider like AWS provides a service level agreement (SLA) of 99.95 percent per zone. An SLA of 99.95 percent equates to 20 minutes and 9 seconds of downtime a month or roughly 4 hours a year. In 2011, a study by Emerson Network Power reported the impact of downtime on the average business equated to a loss of $5,000 a minute or $300,000 an hour.

Apply that number to the 4 hours of downtime a year predicted by the AWS SLA and the average business is looking at $1.2 million of lost business a year! What company in its right mind would not build redundancy across the availability zones knowing the potential losses of a single zone failure? AWS provides multiple zones within a region and multiple regions across the globe. Customers have the opportunity to achieve SLAs far beyond the 99.95 percent by building cross-zone redundancy and/or cross-region redundancy. Everything fails eventually. If AWS takes a hit for two hours, who is really to blame when the customer's website goes down because it did not design for failure? Don't blame the cloud provider; blame the architecture.

Recommendation: When choosing a cloud service model and cloud service providers, understand the risks and points of failure and design for failure. Understand the cloud providers' SLAs, data ownership policies, and thoroughly examine all legal binding documents and agreements. Each cloud service creates some level of vendor lock-in. Study the cause and effect of lock-in and make decisions at the service level. The cloud is not an all-or-nothing proposition. There is no need to be all in or all out. Choose wisely; architect even more wisely.

Underestimating the Impacts of Organizational Change

For a start-up beginning with a blank sheet of paper and building new systems, the cloud has few barriers. For established organizations with existing infrastructure and IT staffs with limited experience in the cloud, the impacts of organizational change should not be underestimated. Change goes way beyond IT, though. Business processes, accounting principles, human resource incentive programs, and legal processes have never had to deal with data and services existing outside of the enterprise. Procurement processes change from buying physical assets and software licenses to paying for virtual infrastructure and on-demand software. Capacity planning changes from the science of forecasting usage in the future to the science of real-time autoscaling. Security now takes center stage and securing data outside of the corporate firewall presents new challenges. The list goes on. Organizations that think of cloud computing as just another IT thing are in for a big surprise.

For some companies, their first attempt at cloud computing might be a proof-of-concept, a research and development exercise, or maybe a low-risk initiative like storing some noncritical data with a cloud storage provider. Small initiatives like these do not create large amounts of organizational change, which lowers the risk of failure. It is when companies take on larger projects or projects that create more risks that they need to implement a plan to manage organizational change.

AEA CASE STUDY: **Dealing with Change**

To give a common example of how organizational change can impact cloud computing initiatives, let's reintroduce our fictitious online auction company Acme eAuctions (AEA).

AEA built an internal customer relationship management (CRM) system nearly 10 years ago to support its on-premises web-based auction platform. Several members of the team that worked on the application are still employed at AEA today and are very proud of their work. However, as the years have passed the application has become increasingly expensive to manage and maintain and does not provide many of the features that a modern CRM tool has today, such as a mobile application, integration with third-party tools, social networking, and more. AEA has decided to move to a SaaS-based CRM solution and the IT team is fighting the decision. They are quoting articles and blog posts about problems with security and uptime in the cloud. The security team is struggling with the concept of putting customer data in the cloud. The SaaS vendor could have the solution turned on and configured in one day, but the effort to export the data out of the legacy system and into the new SaaS-based system is blocking the project. What should be a quick-and-easy win for IT has become a battle between the business and IT. How could AEA have avoided this conflict and the long project delays that the conflict has created?

The conflict is not a technology problem; it is a people problem. We have seen this pattern over and over though the years, whether people were resisting moving off of the mainframe to the client-server model, or pushing back on the enterprise use of the Internet, or refusing to embrace changes in business processes. The bottom line is when people are *told* to change, often their first response is to resist that change. We will discuss strategies for managing change and discuss how AEA addressed the organizational issues to get the project moving forward in Chapter 15 ("Assessing the Organizational Impact of the Cloud Model").

Recommendation: If possible, start with smaller, lower-risk initiatives as the early candidates for cloud computing projects. If the projects are risky and large in size, do not underestimate the impacts of organizational change. Assign somebody as the change leader. That person can be internal or external. Create a sense of urgency, form and empower a team to own the project, create a vision of the future state, and drive that message throughout the organization over and over using every communication mechanism possible (town hall meetings, blogs, newsletters, meetings, posters, etc.).

Skills Shortage

Enterprises often don't have the required expertise to build cloud-based solutions. The average medium-to-large company that has been in business for more than a few years typically has a collection of applications and services spanning multiple eras of application architecture from mainframe to client-server to commercial-off the-shelf and more. The majority of the skills internally are specialized around these different architectures. Often the system administrators and security experts have spent a lifetime working on physical hardware or on-premises virtualization. Cloud architectures are loosely coupled and stateless, which is not how most legacy applications have been built over the years. Many cloud initiatives require integrating with multiple cloud-based solutions from other vendors, partners, and customers. The methods used to test and deploy cloud-based solutions may be radically different and more agile than what companies are accustomed to in their legacy environments. Companies making a move to the cloud should realize that there is more to it than simply deploying or paying for software from a cloud vendor. There are significant changes from an architectural, business process, and people perspective. Often, the skills required to do it right do not exist within the enterprise.

Many legacy architectures have applications that depend on state, as mentioned earlier in this chapter. Building software for the cloud requires developing stateless applications. The secret to well-architected cloud services is to fully understand and embrace the concepts of RESTful services.* Many companies claim that they have service-oriented architectures (SOAs) but many implementations of Representational State Transfer (REST)–based SOA are nothing more than just a bunch of web services (JABOWS). Building RESTful services correctly requires exceptional engineers who know how to architect services in a manner that leverages the virtual compute resources in the cloud. If the developers building solutions in the cloud do not correctly handle the application state, do not provide the correct level of abstraction, and do not apply the right level of granularity, the cloud experience for that company will not be a pleasurable one. Another area where skills tend to fall short is in application security. Companies have built software for years that has lacked the appropriate level of application security. The applications often get by because the perimeter security might be good enough to keep most attacks out. Writing software to run in the cloud outside of the corporate

---

*Thomas Earl states that "statelessness is a preferred condition for services and one that promotes reusability and scalability." These are fundamental characteristics of cloud services.

firewall requires developers and architects who are highly knowledgeable about application security. On the system administration side, development skills are a higher priority in the cloud. Since many manual management tasks are now available as cloud services, administrators need to develop software in conjunction with the application development team. This also requires that administrators use similar application development tools and processes and become part of the release management lifecycle. In many companies application development and system administration do not work closely together and have entirely different skill sets. We will discuss the working relationship between development and operations in detail in Chapter 14 ("Leveraging a DevOps Culture to Deliver Software Faster and More Reliably").

Deploying, monitoring, and maintaining software in the cloud can be drastically different from how an organization currently handles those tasks. Whether developers, administrators, help desk staff, scrum masters, or whatever their role, these people need to have a solid understanding of cloud computing to excel in their jobs. They will need to have a broad knowledge of networking, security, distributed computing, SOA, web architectures, and much more. This change is no different from what happened when organizations shifted from mainframes to client-server architectures. People need to learn new methods in order to make the transition. At the same time, the company needs to keep the lights on and maintain the legacy systems. It is hard to find people who know all the different architectures from the old legacy approaches to the new cloud-based approaches. It can be a good strategy to bring in new staff with experience in the cloud and to help transform the organization and train the existing staff along the way. Trying to move to the cloud with people who are not experienced in cloud architectures will most likely not produce the best results.

Recommendation: Evaluate the current staff and identify skill gaps based on the project requirements. Plug those skill gaps with experienced talent, either full time or contract resources. Make sure the existing staff learns from the experienced people along the way. If only experienced people from the outside get to work on these initiatives, there could be a lot of resentment from within. Attend meet-ups and conferences where practitioners present (beware of vendor pitches), and reach out to local organizations that have had success in the cloud. Encourage team members to take courses, read blogs, and collaborate through their networks to learn about the other people's experiences.

Misunderstanding Customer Requirements

Sometimes IT people neglect the business side of the equation and build the cloud solution that is best for IT. It is critical that part of the service model selection is based on customers' needs. For example, if a company is building an

SaaS solution that is processing credit card information, the business requirements will be drastically different than if the company is building a sports news website. If a company is processing patient health records or top secret government information, the business requirements around security and privacy are far greater than if the company is building a streaming video product.

The details of the business requirements should drive which type of cloud deployment model (public, private, hybrid) and which type of service model (IaaS, PaaS, SaaS) to architect the solution on. If a company is building consumer-facing websites where users voluntarily exchange their personal data for a free service (Facebook, Twitter, Instagram, etc.), the company can easily justify putting everything in a public cloud. If a company is selling to enterprises such as retail establishments, hospitals, and government agencies, there is a very good chance that some customers will demand that at least some of the data is either in a private cloud or does not leave their premises. It is critical to know what the end-user requirements are when it comes to things like security, privacy, integration, regulatory constraints, and so forth. We will discuss these patterns in detail in Chapter 4 ("It Starts with Architecture"). If a company is building SaaS solutions, it should expect customers to demand the highest levels of security, privacy, and auditability requirements. SaaS software has to be secure, reliable, scalable, and configurable or many customers won't buy it. It is key to understand customers' expectations up front so their needs can be built into the underlying architecture from the start.

Recommendation: Understand the business requirements and customer expectations of cloud computing before selecting cloud service models and cloud types. Requirements drive the decisions; the decisions should not drive the requirements. Get clarity on the product definition and requirements, perform a security and regulatory assessment of the requirements, and add the gaps to the overall product backlog. Have a list of frequently asked questions handy that answers all of the questions and concerns that the typical customer will have for the cloud-based solution.

Unexpected Costs

One of the promises of cloud computing is that the pay-as-you-go model greatly reduces the cost of IT infrastructure. This only holds true if the software is architected and managed in a way that optimizes the use of cloud services. One of the powerful things about cloud computing is how quickly services or computing resources can be turned on, but if the process of consuming cloud resources is not closely governed, then the monthly costs can skyrocket, earning you a visit to the CFO's office to explain why you just destroyed her monthly forecast.

Each cloud service model brings a unique set of challenges for controlling costs. SaaS companies typically charge per user or by tier. For example, GitHub, a SaaS-based code repository, has tiers that range from free for public repositories, a Micro tier for up to five repositories for a minimal monthly fee, and several other tiers all the way to the Platinum plan that allows over 125 repositories for $200 a month.* Often these tools are left ungoverned and a company that should be using the Silver plan with 20 repositories at $50 a month is paying $200 for the Platinum and has no idea what repositories exist, who manages them, and which ones are even still being used. Some SaaS solutions charge monthly by user; others are transaction based. Transaction-based SaaS solutions like an e-mail campaign management tool charge per e-mail sent. Some companies use the e-mail tool's APIs and integrate them into their products. If they don't build in safeguards to protect from erroneous code like an infinite loop or a miscalculation, the end results could be a monthly bill that is thousands of dollars higher than expected. Make sure these risks are identified and throttles are built into the system to protect against such scenarios.

PaaS solutions have their share of challenges as well, when it comes to optimizing costs. One of the big benefits of PaaS is that the platforms handle scaling during peak times. The promise of PaaS is that it allows developers to focus on business requirements while the platform handles the infrastructure. Just as in the previous SaaS example, controls must be put in place to ensure that software bugs or even unexpected excessive workloads do not result in the PaaS consuming huge amounts of infrastructure and running up an enormous bill for the month.

IaaS solutions are even more critical to govern closely. It is so easy to deploy a virtual compute resource that without the right controls in place a company can quickly get into a "server sprawl" situation where hundreds of servers are running in various developer and R&D environments and the meter is running on them 24/7. To make matters worse, many of these servers will have dependencies on them that make them hard to shut off. One of my clients was a start-up with a small group of developers who managed everything manually. It worked well because each person was responsible for his own area and it was easy to track all of the virtual servers and what their dependencies were. The small start-up was purchased by a big company and many people were added to the team. No time was allocated to build in processes around managing compute resources and almost overnight the number of servers quadrupled. To make matters worse, nobody was really aware of the impact until finance noticed that the bill was starting to get enormous.

---

*GitHub's cost as of May 2013.

Unfortunately, a number of months had passed before this was noticed, and many of the compute resources had dependencies within the software lifecycle. Each project had one-to-many development, test, quality assurance, and stage environments, and they did not all have the same versions of patches and updates on them. When finance demanded that the team reduce costs, it took several months to take inventory and implement a plan to consolidate and standardize environments. To this day, that client believes that the cloud is more expensive than on-premises computing and is looking for ways to do less in the public cloud. The real issue with costs was a lack of governance, not the cost of cloud computing in public clouds.

The most expensive part of cloud computing usually has nothing to do with the cloud at all. Often, companies underestimate the effort it takes to build software in the cloud. In February 2013, KPMG International published a survey taken by 650 executives worldwide on the adoption of cloud computing. The survey found that one-third of the respondents discovered that costs related to their cloud computing initiatives were higher than they expected. The respondents pointed to a lack of in-house skills and complexities with integrating to existing systems as some of the main reasons for the inflated costs. With the right architecture and governance, cloud computing can drive down costs substantially within an organization, but there are no shortcuts or magic pills that will guarantee that success. At the end of the day it comes down to architecture and planning. In Chapter 4 ("It Starts with Architecture"), we will discuss this in more detail.

Recommendation: Understand the costs of each cloud service model and establish the appropriate levels of governance and software controls to optimize and monitor costs. For companies with legacy solutions, don't underestimate the effort required to integrate with legacy architectures and the costs of training existing employees or hiring experienced engineers.

Summary

The reality is that implementing cloud initiatives can be much more challenging than many people are led to believe. Companies that successfully implement cloud initiatives can reduce IT costs, improve speed to market, and focus more on their core competencies. Start-ups have the luxury of building from scratch for the cloud, but established companies have both legacy solutions and legacy IT shops that may require significant changes in order to have success moving to the cloud. Companies attempting to build in the cloud should become aware of the worst practices mentioned in this chapter and pay attention to the recommendations. The marketing hype from the vendors makes cloud computing initiatives seem incredibly easy. Don't be fooled by their PowerPoint slides. It is critical that a company fully understands the pros and cons of each service model and the implications pertaining to key issues such as security, privacy, data ownership, regulations, costs, impact of organization change, and much more.

References

Bennett, C., and A. Tseitlin (2012, July 30). "Chaos Monkey Released into the Wild." Retrieved from http://techblog.netflix.com/2012/07/chaos-monkey-released-into-wild.html.

Cloud Security Alliance. 2011. "Security Guidance for Critical Areas of Focus in Cloud Computing v3.0." General format, retrieved from https://cloudsecurity alliance.org/guidance/csaguide.v3.0.pdf.

Erl, Thomas. 2008. *Service-Oriented Architecture: Concepts, Technology, and Design*. Boston, MA: Prentice Hall.

Hill, S., and R. Wright (2013, February). "The Cloud Takes Shape: Global Cloud Survey: The Implementation Challenge." Retrieved from http://www.kpmg.com/Global/en/IssuesAndInsights/ArticlesPublications/cloud-service-providers-survey/Documents/the-cloud-takes-shapev2.pdf.

Hoff, T. (2012, April 9). "The Instagram Architecture that Facebook Bought for a Cool Billion Dollars." Retrieved from http://highscalability.com/blog/2012/4/9/the-instagram-architecture-facebook-bought-for-a-cool-billio.html.

Johnson, R. (2011, July 5). "Army's $2.7 Billion Cloud Computing System Does Not Work." Retrieved from http://www.rawstory.com/rs/2011/07/05/armys-2–7-billion-cloud-computing-system-does-not-work/.

Linthicum, David S. 2009. *Cloud Computing and SOA Convergence in Your Enterprise: A Step-by-Step Guide*. Boston, MA: Addison-Wesley.

n.a. (2012, September 27). "Cyber Security: 75% of Data Breaches Are Inside Jobs." Retrieved from http://www.theinformationdaily.com/2012/09/27/75-of-data-breaches-are-inside-jobs.

Preimesberger, C. (2011, May 13). "Unplanned IT Downtime Can Cost $5K per Minute: Report." Retrieved from http://www.eweek.com/c/a/IT-Infrastructure/Unplanned-IT-Downtime-Can-Cost-5K-Per-Minute-Report-549007/.

Wainewright, P. (2009, February 3). "Coghead's Demise Highlights PaaS Lock-out Risk." Retrieved from http://www.zdnet.com/blog/saas/cogheads-demise-highlights-paas-lock-out-risk/668.

CHAPTER 4

It Starts with Architecture

A doctor can bury his mistakes but an architect can only advise his clients to plant vines.

—FRANK LLOYD WRIGHT, U.S. ARCHITECT

When constructing a house, nobody would ever consider not buying materials and tools and hiring resources as the first steps of the building process. Yet, too often in the world of IT we see teams rush to the development phase without a clear vision of what the business and technical requirements are. With cloud computing, the need for a pragmatic approach is even more critical because the risks are greater as more control is shifted to cloud service providers. Whether a company has an official enterprise architecture practice in place or not, success in the cloud is dependent on applying the basics of sound architectural principles and asking these six questions: *Why, Who, What, Where, When*, and *How*.

The Importance of Why, Who, What, Where, When, and How

There have been philosophical debates for decades on the value of enterprise architecture (EA). Architecting for the cloud does not require that an official EA organization exists within a company or that any formal EA methodology like The Open Group Architecture Framework (TOGAF) or the Zachman Framework is used. However, architects should perform the necessary discovery steps that most methodologies suggest before diving headfirst into the clouds. A mistake that many companies make is picking a vendor before doing their due diligence. It is easy for a Microsoft shop to automatically default to Microsoft's Azure even though Platform as a Service (PaaS) might not be the best service model to solve the business challenge. Architects should seek answers to the following questions:

Why. What problem are we trying to solve? What are the business goals and drivers?

Who. Who needs this problem solved? Who are all the actors involved (internal/external)?

What. What are the business and technical requirements? What legal and/or regulatory constraints apply? What are the risks?

Where. Where will these services be consumed? Are there any location-specific requirements (regulations, taxes, usability concerns, language/locale issues, etc.)?

When. When are these services needed? What is the budget? Are there dependencies on other projects/initiatives?

The final question to ask is often overlooked, even though it is one of the most important questions. This question focuses on the current state of the organization and its ability to adapt to the changes that cloud computing brings.

How. How can the organization deliver these services? What is the readiness of the organization, the architecture, the customer?

After collecting the information for these questions, architects are in a better position to select the best service model(s) and deployment model(s) for their company. In Chapter 5, "Choosing the Right Cloud Service Model," we will see how factors like time, budget, and organizational readiness can impact the cloud service model decisions just as much as the business and technical requirements. Other factors that can contribute to the cloud service model and deployment model decisions are whether the project is a greenfield effort being built from scratch from the ground up, a migration of a legacy system, or a combination of the two. Legacy systems can create barriers that make it difficult to use certain cloud service models and deployment models. There are many cloud service providers that offer migration services that should be evaluated if a cloud migration is considered.

The types of users and data have an impact on the cloud architecture, as well. For example, a social networking website where consumers opt in and agree to share their data has very different requirements from a health application capturing and storing medical records for cancer patients. The latter has many more constraints, risks, and regulatory requirements that most likely will result in a very different cloud architecture from the social network platform. We will discuss these decision points in detail in the next chapter.

Start with the Business Architecture

A good first step when starting a major cloud initiative is to create a business architecture diagram. This is important because it provides insights into the various touchpoints and business functions across the enterprise or at least across the part of the enterprise that is in scope for the initiative.

AEA CASE STUDY: **Business Architecture Viewpoint**

Our fictitious online auction company, Acme eAuctions (AEA), is considering moving its auction platform to the cloud. Its original platform was built in-house several years ago, before cloud computing was a popular concept. AEA has been very successful over the years, but the platform is showing its age and the company is spending too much money just keeping the platform stable, leaving very little time to deliver enhancements such as mobile, social, and rich media functionality. AEA has received approval from the board to build a new platform and believes that leveraging the cloud can help it achieve scale at a lower price point while delivering with greater speed to market. Before diving into the new platform, AEA wisely mapped out its future state business architecture as shown in Figure 4.1.

Using this diagram, the team can see the various points of integration and endpoints within the architecture. Across the top of the diagram, AEA clearly defines who the external actors are in the system and the different touchpoints that users will use to interact with the system. All external access will come through the application programming interface (API) layer. AEA has defined six core business processes that make up the workflow of a product, from its inception to the sale to the close of the transaction. Underneath the business processes are a collection of services. There are services in support of the buyers and another set of services for the sellers. Underneath those services are a collection of shared business services that are used by both buyers and sellers. Underneath those services are utility services such as security, events, and notifications. The bottom layer shows integration points to several other enterprise systems that this platform will feed.

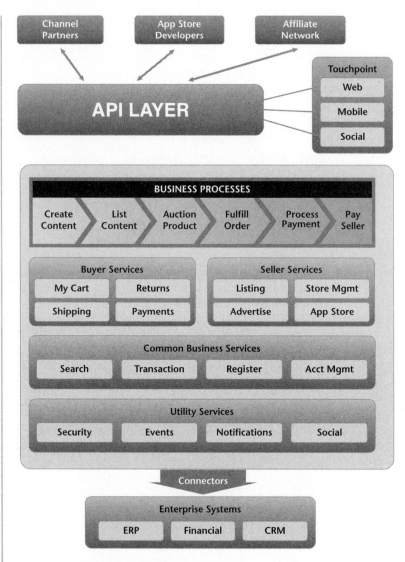

Figure 4.1   Business Architecture

Even though the first phase of the project may only focus on a single component of the architecture, it is important to understand how that component fits into the entire business architecture. Too often we build things with a limited view of the enterprise and wind up deploying solutions that are difficult to integrate within the enterprise. It is like planning to install a door in the front entrance with a limited understanding of what the rest of the house looks like. Sure, we can successfully install the door within the doorframe, but what if the door opens out and we did not know that another worker was putting a screen door in front of the door? It doesn't matter if the screen door is getting installed now or a year from now; either way we would have to replace the original door to open in. The same applies to building cloud services. The architects should have some level of visibility into the overall vision of the enterprise before they start installing doors.

AEA CASE STUDY: Defining the Business Problem Statement

AEA's existing auction site is built of many proprietary components. The goal of the new architecture is to create an open platform and expose an API layer so that channel partners, app store developers, and affiliate network partners can connect seamlessly to the auction platform. AEA wants to create an Auction PaaS. It will provide all of the infrastructure and application logic for running auctions so other companies can build content on top of this platform. This approach brings more sellers and buyers to the AEA platform, thereby increasing revenue. In the old model, AEA had a large sales force that focused on attracting sellers and buyers to sign up on the AEA website. The new model allows companies that have merchandise to set up virtual stores and run auctions on top of the AEA platform. In addition, AEA wants to modernize its platform to include mobile and social features. It believes mobile will increase transactions, and social media is a great method of getting its brand name out to its customers' networks. Transactions through its API layer equate to new revenue streams that are not available in its current architecture.

In the new architecture, AEA is commited to a service-oriented architecture (SOA). Most of its legacy architecture was built in silos over the years and is made up of many different technology stacks, including Java, .NET, and PHP. The company currently has two data centers, both at about 80 percent capacity. Senior management does not want to expand or invest in any more physical data centers and has asked for at least a 20 percent reduction in infrastructure costs. The team has until the end of the year to enable the integration with channel partners, app store developers, and the affiliate network. The anticipated revenue from this new integration is what has justified this project, so it is critical that the date is met (they have six months to make this happen).

AEA CASE STUDY: **Pragmatic Approach**

Jamie Jacobson, the lead architect on the project, starts to answer the six key questions as a first step. AEA uses an agile methodology, but it understands that there are some necessary discovery steps that must take place before the team starts building solutions. In fact, with the tight timeline, it is highly likely that they will have to leverage SaaS, PaaS, or IaaS solutions in many areas as opposed to building things themselves if they are to have a prayer of hitting the date. Here are Jamie's notes:

Why. Create open platform to enable new revenue streams.
Reduce data center footprint and infrastructure costs.
Mobile and social to attract customers, drive more traffic.

Who. AEA needs this to stay competitive.
New actors: channel partners, app store developers, affiliate network.
Data center operations need to modernize and reduce infrastructure.

What. Need stronger security now that system is exposed to third parties.
Need to connect to partners' fulfillment and shipping partners.
Must protect/secure all transactions; possible client audits.
Must scale to handle random spikes in traffic.

Where. Geographic rules for selling products (age, taxes).
Buyers and sellers can live in any country.

When. Third-party integration by end of year (six months).

How. Limited IT experience in cloud and SOA.
Operating model is significantly different—never supported third parties before.

The next step for Jamie and the team is to recommend an architecture to accomplish these goals. They call this effort *Sprint 0*. The first sprint, which they decided would be one week long, is to take the six questions and iterate though them to get enough detail to start another architecture sprint. In the second architecture sprint the architect team needs to accomplish these goals:

- Research cloud computing.
- Propose an architecture for the immediate goal of integrating with third parties with the long-term goal of delivering an auction PaaS.
- Determine nonfunctional requirements for the platform.

AEA is off to a good start, but there is much work to do. Sprint 0 is a critical discovery exercise. The team needs to gather a lot of information fast and a task force should be assigned to assess the organizational impacts. As we approach as they deal wit progress through this book, Jamie and the team will continue their pragmatic h issues like security, data, service level agreements, scaling, and more.

Identify the Problem Statement (Why)

The question, "What problem are we trying to solve?" (the *why*) is the single most important question to answer. What are the business drivers for leveraging cloud computing services within an organization? The answer is different for every company, every culture, and every architecture. For example, for start-ups, building new in the cloud is a no-brainer. In fact, if a start-up decides to build and manage its own infrastructure, it better have a very compelling reason for selecting physical infrastructure and data centers over cloud computing, because most venture capitalists (VC) and angel investors will question the management team's leadership.

On the other side of the equation are large established enterprises with huge amounts of physical infrastructure on the balance sheets and many different technology stacks and legacy architectures deployed in production environments. Figuring out how to best leverage cloud services is a much more complicated decision to make in enterprises. If one of the business drivers is to "reduce IT infrastructure costs," a start-up can easily achieve that goal by building its greenfield applications in the cloud without investing in data centers and infrastructure and all the people to manage them. An established enterprise will have to evaluate every single component of the existing enterprise separately to determine what can be moved to the cloud and which deployment model (public, private, hybrid) makes sense for each component.

A large organization may choose to reduce costs many different ways and leverage different service models. For example, it may be supporting numerous commercial software products to manage noncore competency business processes like payroll, human resources tasks, accounting, and so forth. The organization may decide to replace these solutions with Software as a Service (SaaS) solutions. At the same time it may not be as easy to migrate legacy applications to a PaaS or an Infrastructure as a Service (IaaS) cloud provider because the underlying architecture does not support web-based or stateless architectures and the cost of rearchitecting makes it unfeasible. Instead, the organization may choose to leverage the cloud for specific purposes like backup and recovery, provisioning testing and development environments on demand, or integrating with an external API for a specific set of data (maps, Zip code lookups, credit check, etc.). Every piece of the overall architecture should be evaluated independently to ensure that the optimal cloud service and deployment models are selected. With the exception of greenfield start-ups, rarely does it make sense to select one cloud service model and one deployment model. Use a hammer when you have nails and a screwdriver when you have screws.

Evaluate User Characteristics (Who)

The *who* question identifies the users of the system, both internal and external. Users may be people or systems. Identifying the actors helps discover what organizations (internal and external) interact with the overall system. Each actor within a system may have its own unique needs. It is possible that one cloud service model does not meet the needs of every actor.

AEA CASE STUDY: Multiple Cloud Service Models

In the AEA business architecture diagram, there are consumers interfacing with a high-scale website and there are suppliers interfacing with an inventory system. If AEA wants to scale to eBay levels, it may choose the IaaS service model so it has more control over the overall performance and scalability of the system. For the inventory system, it may choose to migrate to a SaaS solution. The key takeaway is that an enterprise often leverages multiple cloud service models to meet the needs of the various actors within a system.

Once the actors are identified, it is important to understand the characteristics of these actors, such as demographics (age group, how tech savvy they are, what countries they are in, etc.), type of actor (person, business, government, etc.), type of business (social media, health, manufacturing, etc.), and so forth. The who question uncovers numerous functional and nonfuntional requirements. In the case of cloud computing, actor characteristics drive important design considerations in the areas of privacy, regulations, usability, risk, and more.

Identify Business and Technical Requirements (What)

The *what* question drives the discovery of many functional and nonfunctional requirements. Functional requirements describe how the system, application, or service should function. Functional requirements describe the following:

- What data the system must process.
- How the screens should operate.
- How the workflow operates.

- What the outputs of the system are.
- Who has access to each part of the system.
- What regulations must be adhered to.

Nonfunctional requirements describe how the architecture functions. The following list contains the categories of nonfunctional requirements that should be evaluated to assist in selecting the appropriate cloud service and deployment models:

- **Usability**. Requirements for end users and systems that use the platform.
- **Performance**. Ability to respond to user and system requests.
- **Flexibility**. Ability to change at the speed of business with minimal code changes.
- **Capability**. Ability to perform business functions both current and future.
- **Security**. Requirements around security, privacy, and compliance.
- **Traceability**. Requirements around logging, auditing, notifications, and event processing.
- **Reusability**. Level of reuse required both internally and externally.
- **Integrability**. Ability to integrate with various systems and technologies.
- **Standardization**. Specific industry standards to comply with.
- **Scalability**. Ability to scale to meet demands of the business.
- **Portability**. Capability to deploy on various hardware and software platforms.
- **Reliability**. Required uptime and SLAs, along with recovery mechanisms.

Visualize the Service Consumer Experience (Where)

A good building architect would never build a plan for a house if he had no idea where the house was going to be located, how big the lot is, what the zoning restrictions are, what the climate is like, and all of those constraints that come with the location of the building. For example, in Florida, much of the architecture of a house focuses on withstanding high winds during hurricane season and extreme heat during the summer. The architecture for a new house in Toronto will likely avoid the design costs associated with withstanding hurricane-force winds but instead focus more on holding up to cold temperatures and distributing heat evenly throughout the structure.

With cloud computing, it is critical to understand the impact of laws as they relate to the locale where the cloud services are being consumed and where the data is being stored. Laws and regulations have different constraints across countries, provinces, states, and even counties. For example, in the couponing industry, marketing campaigns focusing on tobacco, alcohol, and even dairy must comply with laws against promoting these categories within certain counties.

The 2013 *Global Cloud Computing Report Card*, published by Business Software Alliance (BSA), stated, "Cloud services operate across national boundaries, and their success depends on access to regional and global markets. Restrictive policies that create actual or potential trade barriers will slow the evolution of cloud computing." Some countries, like Japan, have modernized their legislation around privacy law, criminal law, and IP protection to facilitate the digital economy and cloud computing. On the other end of the spectrum are countries, like China, that have complex laws that discriminate against foreign technology companies and restrict the types of data that can flow in and out of the country. Countries that have restrictions on data transfers outside of their country create challenges for technology companies trying to build cloud solutions.

Perhaps one of the most controversial laws impacting cloud computing is the USA Patriot Act of 2001. The Patriot Act was signed into law shortly after the 9/11 terrorist attacks on the World Trade Center in New York City. This new legislation gave the U.S. law enforcement and intelligence agencies the ability to inspect digital data from any U.S. company or any company that conducts business in the United States. Many non-U.S. countries storing sensitive data fear that the U.S. government might seize their data and therefore choose to store their data in-house and opt out of the cloud. What many people don't know is that many countries have similar laws that give their intelligence agencies the same type of power and access that the Patriot Act has in order to help protect against terrorism.

Architects need to become familiar with the laws and regulations that pertain to their business and their data. The impact of these laws can influence decisions like public versus private cloud, cloud versus noncloud, and local vendor versus international vendor. Often, hybrid cloud solutions are used to address these concerns. Companies often leverage public IaaS or PaaS service models for the majority of their processing needs and keep the data they do not want subject to seizure under laws like the Patriot Act in a private cloud or in an in-house noncloud data center.

A more exciting *where* question is: What devices and touchpoints are these cloud services being accessed by? Today's users consume data through channels on many touchpoints. We consume information on the web, on mobile devices and tablets, with scanners, and with medical devices, to name a few. Even our cars, refrigerators, home security systems, and almost anything with an IP address can interact with end users in this day and age. Knowing up front what all of these touchpoints are can drive some important decisions.

AEA CASE STUDY: **Mobile Development Decision**

Let's assume AEA plans to allow users to access its auction site on smart phones and feature phones, tablets, PCs, and laptops and also publish its APIs so that other website properties can embed AEA auctions within their sites. A lot of development is required to support all of those different touchpoints, browser versions, and third-party websites, which likely are written in a variety of languages, like .NET, PHP, Python, and so on. AEA may choose a PaaS solution specializing in mobile devices and tablets to expedite and simplify the development process. These platforms are sometimes referred to as *Mobile Backend as a Service* (mBaaS) and focus on allowing the developers to build one code base that can run seamlessly across multiple device types and browser versions.

SaaS vendors like Apigee, Mashery, and Layer 7 Technologies provide cloud services for building APIs to publish to third parties. These SaaS tools provide security, transformation, routing, web and mobile analytics, and many other important services that allow the developers to focus on their business requirements. Like the mobile PaaS tools, the API SaaS tools increase the developers' speed to market and reduce maintenance because the vendors take care of supporting new technologies, standards, and patterns. For example, if a new device becomes popular or a change is made to a standard like OAuth, the mobile PaaS and API SaaS vendors update their products, allowing the developers to focus on their business needs.

Identify the Project Constraints (When and with What)

It is important to understand the budget and the expected delivery dates. Time may be a critical factor in choosing cloud service models. If there is a business reason to implement a new CRM solution in the next month, then leveraging a SaaS solution is probably the only way to meet that time constraint. Sometimes dates are artificially assigned. How many times have we seen projects with a January 1 due date? Usually there is no business driver for this date other than somebody is assigned a goal and objective to deliver a project by year-end. But other times dates are critical to the business. For example, a business that generates most of its revenues before the Thanksgiving and Christmas holidays may have an urgent need to deliver a new product or service or improve the overall system performance before the traffic peaks. In either case, the date is critical to the business's bottom line. Regardless of whether the time constraint is real or artificial, it is a constraint that must be taken into consideration when making architecture decisions. Sometimes what is best for the architecture is not best for the business. It is critical that all architecture decisions are made with business goals in mind first and foremost.

There may be other constraints that impact the cloud service and deployment models. Management or customers may create artificial constraints. For example, they may dictate, without performing the proper due diligence, that all public cloud options are off-limits. Whether that decision is good or bad, it is a constraint that can be accounted for and the focus can shift to private cloud and SaaS solutions. A company might decide it wants to drastically reduce its infrastructure footprint and reduce the number of its data centers. In this case, architects should look at public cloud options as well as SaaS and PaaS options. Another scenario may be that there is a mandate to use a certain vendor. Whatever the constraints are, it is important to identify them up front before major decisions are made.

Understand Current State Constraints (How)

Organizational readiness is the main theme when asking the *how* questions. Does the company have the skills in-house? Are accounting and finance willing and able to shift from a capital expenditure (buying up front) model to an operational expenditure (pay-as-you-go) model? What is the mind-set of the culture? Are they resisisting the change? Are they capable of change?

Organizational change management is critical to the success of any transformational change initiative within a company. Whether a company is trying to implement a new business strategy, a new development methodology, or adopt new technologies, there is always the element of organizational change that must be addressed. In many cases, the change is more challenging than the new technology or the new strategy that is being implemented.

People need to understand why change is necessary and how that change will improve things in the future. John Kotter, the author of numerous books on organizational change management, categorized the following eight errors common to organizational change efforts:

1. Allowing too much complacency
2. Failing to create a powerful guiding coalition
3. Underestimating the importance of a vision
4. Undercommunicating the vision
5. Allowing obstacles to block the vision
6. Failing to create short wins
7. Declaring victory too soon
8. Neglecting to make changes part of corporate culture

A common mistake that I have seen through the years is that companies often neglect to involve human resources (HR) in the process. New initiatives often require a change in behaviors, but if the HR processes still reward the old behaviors and do nothing to encourage the new desired behaviors, then there are no incentives for employees to change.

AEA CASE STUDY: Dealing with Change

John Stanford is the vice president of Infrastructure at AEA. He started at AEA 15 years ago as a systems administrator and worked his way up to his current position. He has hired many of the people on his current staff, including the two security experts that report to him. Many of the people on John's team are not supportive of the company's goal to leverage the cloud for the new platform. They continue to raise issues about security, stability, and lack of control that come with the cloud. John manages the budget for all of the infrastructure and is already planning for a new project to expand to another data center in two years because the current data center is nearing capacity. John is well aware of the costs and the incredible amount of labor required to build out another data center. Leveraging the cloud seems to make a lot of sense to John, but how can he get his people on board?

John starts holding one-on-one meetings with his staff members to discuss their thoughts on cloud computing. What he discovers is that many of his staff members are afraid that their jobs might be going away. When John explains the business benefits of leveraging the cloud, the staff immediately shifts focus to building a private cloud regardless if that deployment model is the best fit for the business. John realizes he needs to provide a new set of incentives in order to motivate his staff differently. So John challenges them to reduce costs of archiving all of the back-office applications by 50 percent over the next six months. He gives them a directive to eliminate tape and disk backup and move all backups for these systems to a cloud storage solution. By giving his staff ownership in the change process and by giving them a project that directly impacts their day-to-day job in a positive way, John increases the odds that his team will adapt over time. Nobody on his team will miss backup tapes and devices. This is a much better introduction to cloud computing than having the development team force them into supporting their cloud aspirations. John changed his staff's incentive to drive the desired outcome. He tied the project to a business objective and made it an achievable goal on their objectives. Now it is up to John to stay on top of his team and continue to drive the change forward.

Companies that have a long legacy of building and deploying on-premises systems are likely to experience resistance within the ranks. No matter how good the IT team may be when it comes to building software, without buy-in throughout the organization, delivering in the cloud will be a challenge. Don't forget to address the *how* question.

Summary

As with implementing any technology, it is highly recommended to focus first on defining the architecture before rushing to decisions on vendors and cloud service models. It is important that the technology decisions are driven mainly from business drivers rather than technology preferences. Ask the *who*, *what*, *why*, *where*, *when*, and *how* questions early in the project so that informed decisions can be made about cloud service models and deployment models. Understand the constraints, both artificial and real, up front before decisions are made. By no way does this recommendation dictate the process in which an organization answers these questions. On the surface it might sound like I am recommending a waterfall approach, which I am not. Agile practitioners can work these discovery tasks into their sprints in any fashion that they like. The point is that these discovery questions should be asked and the answers should have an impact on the design decisions and ultimately the overall architecture.

References

Kendall, K., and J. Kendall (2003). *Systems Analysis and Design*, 6th ed. Upper Saddle River, NJ: Pearson Prentice Hall.

Kotter, John P. (1996). *Leading Change*. Boston: Harvard Business School Press.

Ross, J., P. Weill, and D. Robertson (2006). *Enterprise Architecture as a Strategy: Creating a Foundation for Business Execution*. Boston: Harvard Business School Press.

Ross, J., Weill, P. (2004). *IT Governance: How Top Performers Manage IT Decision Rights for Superior Results*. Boston: Harvard Business School Press.

Schekkerman, Jaap. (2008). *Enterprise Architecture Good Practices Guide: How to Manage the Enterprise Architecture Practice*. Victoria, BC, Canada: Trafford Publishing.

Galexa Consulting. (2013). "BSA Global Cloud Computing Scorecard: A Blueprint for Economic Opportunity." Retrieved from http://portal.bsa.org/cloudscorecard2012/assets/PDFs/BSA_GlobalCloudScorecard.pdf.

Whittaker, Z. (2012, December 4). "Patriot Act Can Obtain Data in Europe, Researchers Say." Retrieved from http://www.cbsnews.com/8301–205_162–57556674/patriot-act-can-obtain-data-in-europe-researchers-say/.

CHAPTER 5

Choosing the Right Cloud Service Model

It takes less time to do things right than to explain why you did it wrong.

—HENRY WADSWORTH LONGFELLOW, POET

One misperception about cloud computing is that one cloud service model fits all. That is the equivalent of choosing one tool to build a house. Obviously, it takes many different tools to build a house because there are so many different components that make up the architecture of the house. There is a concrete foundation; infrastructure items like plumbing, electrical, and sewage; interior items like walls, floors, and windows; and external items like roofs, driveways, gutters, and so on. Each component has its own set of requirements and therefore requires a different collection of tools. Obviously, laying and paving the driveway requires much different tools and processes than installing the plumbing or tiling the floors. It is a no-brainer that building a house requires many different skills and many different tools, and each component of the construction of a house has its own characteristics within the architecture of the entire house.

Building enterprise-grade software in the cloud is no different. Just as a builder uses many different tools and skills to build a house, an enterprise should use different cloud services models within the enterprise. Some companies pick a single cloud provider like Amazon Web Services (AWS), which provides Infrastructure as a Service (IaaS) solutions, or Azure, a provider of Platform as a Service (PaaS) solutions, and force-fit all solutions into that cloud service model whether it makes sense to do so or not. This chapter focuses on explaining what use cases make sense for each cloud service model. Companies that understand the pros and cons of each cloud service model will likely implement solutions on all three.

Considerations When Choosing a Cloud Service Model

In Chapter 1, we discussed the definitions of each cloud service model. Figure 5.1 summarizes each cloud service model.

There are many factors that go into choosing the right service model. Decision makers should consider the feasibility of each cloud service model based on the following five categories:

1. Technical
2. Financial
3. Strategic
4. Organization
5. Risk

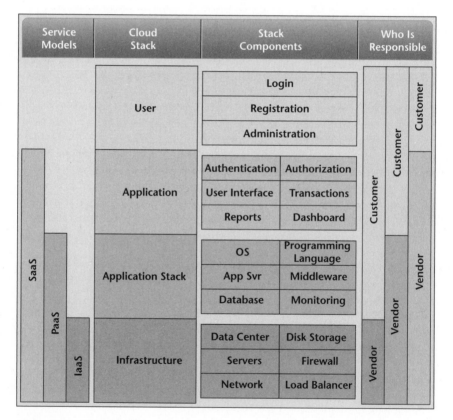

Figure 5.1   Cloud Stack

The *technical* category focuses on areas like performance, scalability, security, regulation, business continuity, disaster recovery, and so on. Performance and scalability requirements are critical for deciding between PaaS and IaaS service models. One of the greatest benefits of PaaS is that platforms abstract the underlying infrastructure from the developer so the developer can focus on business requirements while the platform handles autoscaling. Since PaaS vendors are responsible for scaling all of their tenants, they enforce limitations on the amount of resources that can be requested by a tenant. For most applications, the limitations are set so high they are not a factor, but for applications with an extreme number of transactions, PaaS cannot deliver the performance and scale. Some of the top-visited websites, like Facebook, Twitter, and Pinterest, leverage IaaS cloud service models because they cannot rely on a platform to achieve the scale they must deliver.

Both IaaS and PaaS solutions offer Database as a Service (DBaaS) solutions that automatically manage database management tasks like replication, autoscaling, monitoring, backups, and more. One limitation of DBaaS is the lack of control over the database. My first start-up, M-Dot Network, winner of the 2010 AWS Global Start-Up Challenge, had a unique technical solution for processing digital incentives at point-of-sale (POS) systems. M-Dot partnered with POS vendors to build a message broker that was integrated and shipped with POS software. The message broker sent the shopping orders and items to M-Dot's cloud-based digital incentive platform on AWS. The digital incentive platform would process the incoming data and determine if shoppers qualified to redeem any digital offers that were in their digital wallets. The redemption message was returned to the POS system in subsecond response time. Anyone familiar with the retail industry knows that POS systems require extremely high service level agreements (SLAs) and the worst thing a third party can do is shut down a retailer's POS system. M-Dot wanted to leverage Amazon Relational Database Service (Amazon RDS), Amazon's DBaaS application programming interface (API), to take advantage of the advanced features and automation of database management tasks. However, the consequences of the database going off-line were so great that we chose to manage the database ourselves. This strategy paid off. AWS had a few well-publicized outages, and in several of those outages, RDS was either down or impacted. Because M-Dot chose to manage the database itself, we never missed a POS transaction on any AWS outage even though many popular websites were completely down. It came with a cost, though. We invested a lot of time and money in architecting a fail-over solution that included master–slave and cross-zone redundancy.

The *financial* aspects should focus on total cost of ownership (TCO), which requires a lot more thought than calculating the price per hour or per month of a cloud service. If the project is focused on building new applications, it is much easier to calculate the TCO, but for projects that are migrating solutions to the cloud or are new but are constrained by existing legacy architectures, the TCO is much more complex to calculate. For the latter, decision makers must estimate the cost to change and/or integrate with the legacy architectures. In many cases, moving to the cloud brings costs of retrofitting existing architectures so that they can be integrated with new cloud services. On top of the costs to build new services in the cloud, other costs may include projects to reengineer legacy architectures, employee training, hiring new employees or consultants, acquiring tools or services to assist in reengineering, and much more.

Strategic requirements may come into play as well. The more important speed-to-market is for an initiative, the more likely the decision makers will look to leverage SaaS or PaaS over IaaS simply because much of the IT work is being performed by the cloud service providers, as opposed to an IaaS solution where IT still does a lot of the heavy lifting. If control is the most important strategy, it is more likely that the decision makers will gravitate toward an IaaS solution where IT has more control over the underlying infrastructure, whereas with SaaS and PaaS the infrastructure is abstracted from the end user. Business strategies such as consolidating data centers, reducing costs, being first to market, handling enormous scale, selling product globally 24/7, integrating with partner supply chains, and others all contribute to deciding which cloud service model to select. Too often companies pick a cloud vendor solely based on technical preferences without putting enough weight on the business strategies that are driving the cloud initiatives.

An assessment of the *organization* may play a role in what cloud service model to choose. Does the IT organization have the skills to build solutions in the cloud? If the company does not have strong IT skills in the areas of distributed computing, web development, and service-oriented architectures (SOAs), maybe it should lean more toward SaaS and PaaS service models or find a partner that can build cloud services on IaaS. The lower down the cloud stack the company goes, the higher the degree of competence the staff needs.

The final category is *risk*. How much risk is a company willing to assume? How long can the solution be down? How damaging is a security breach? Can the government seize the data in the cloud with a warrant? There are an endless number of questions to consider when it comes to risk. Risk also is a major determining factor in whether a company chooses to go with a public cloud, a private, or a hybrid of both. Often, areas such as privacy, data ownership, and regulation are very strong factors in the determination of which cloud service model and which deployment model to use.

Every company and even each individual cloud initiative within a company may weight each category differently. For example, a company building a social media site where customers volunteer to post their personal data, like pictures, videos, and so on, will likely put a higher weight on the technical requirements to achieve high scale and uptime and a lower weight on risks, given that nobody dies when your favorite social media site goes down. On the flipside, a medical company responsible for processing medical claims most likely weights the risk category as high as or even higher than most of the others. In the following sections we will discuss use cases for each service model and show some examples of how AEA addresses its key decision points.

When to Use SaaS

Software as a Service is the most mature of the three cloud service models. Early pioneers like Salesforce.com have perfected the execution of delivering complete applications in the cloud that cloud service consumers can access over the Internet with a browser. The SaaS providers have total control over the infrastructure, performance, security, scalability, privacy, and much more. SaaS vendors typically offer two ways for their customers to use their applications. The most common method is a web-based user interface that usually is accessible on any device that can connect to the Internet. The other way is to provide APIs to their customers so service consumers can integrate features into their existing applications or with other SaaS solutions.

A company should use SaaS to outsource all applications, features, and services that are not a core competency, assuming it meets its needs and is affordable. For example, if a company is not in the business of writing HR, payroll, customer relationship management (CRM), and accounting software, it should not build these applications. Buying these applications and running them on-premises is not cost effective with the emergence of SaaS alternatives. Why buy the software and servers, manage the servers, and pay people to manage, patch, secure, and provide other non-value-add tasks to keep these services running?

SaaS solutions fall into many different categories. The most popular are *enterprise business* applications like CRM, enterprise resource planning (ERP), accounting, human resources, and payroll. There are a number of IT *infrastructure* SaaS solutions that deal with security, monitoring, logging, testing, and so on. The *data* category includes business intelligence, database as a service, data visualization, dashboards, data mining, and more. The *productivity* category includes collaboration tools, development tools, surveys, e-mail campaign tools, and much more.

Because SaaS providers cater to many customers they often do not provide the same level of flexibility that a company would have if it built its own application. Sometimes companies choose to build their own applications because there is a feature or a configuration that they want but can't find from the SaaS vendors. Before a company decides to build it itself, it should consider all of the tasks that SaaS vendors perform on their customers' behalf and factor them into the total cost of ownership:

- Vendor is responsible for security updates and patches.
- Vendor manages all infrastructure and data center.
- Vendor usually provides mobile compatibility for majority of phones and tablets.
- Vendor provides compatibility across all major browsers and versions.
- Vendor frequently updates features and updates are seamless to end user.
- Vendor manages databases, including capacity planning, backup recovery, and so on.

Before a company decides to write the application itself, it should compare the value of the feature(s) that the SaaS tools cannot provide against the TCO of building it itself. Another part of the equation is to consider the opportunity cost for shifting the resources to another project or reducing the number of resources to lower costs. Once a company builds an application it must pay ongoing to keep it current and fix bugs. The speed of change in technology is amazingly fast. Can a company continue to invest precious IT resources upgrading legacy applications to work on the next new phone or tablet? When the next social media darling, like Pinterest, appears out of nowhere, can companies quickly react and integrate with the API? To stay current with technology, companies will have to invest a substantial amount of resources to make these upgrades. Every hour spent keeping up with technology changes is an hour a company is not using to build the next new product or an hour it is not using to reduce costs.

AEA CASE STUDY: Use Case for SaaS

Let's take another look at the business architecture for Acme eAuction's future PaaS platform in Figure 5.2.

Here are some of the constraints (organized in the five categories we discussed previously) that Jamie collected in Chapter 4:

1. **Technical**. Dynamic traffic loads from third parties, increase security.
2. **Financial**. Reduce infrastructure costs.
3. **Strategic**. Increase revenue via third-party integration.
4. **Organizational**. Lack of cloud and SOA skills.
5. **Risk**. Must get to market quickly (six months).

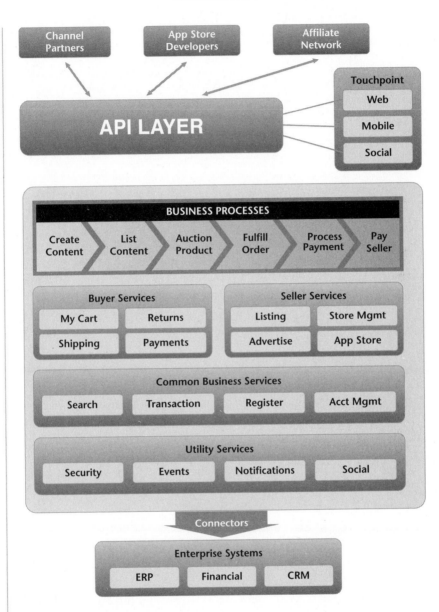

Figure 5.2   Business Architecture

As Jamie looks at the constraints on his project, it is obvious that speed is important. The ROI of the entire initiative is based on an aggressive time frame. Time is a major constraint on the architecture. There is a risk of opportunity costs if the project is late. The team has been asked to reduce the infrastructure footprint. Another critical constraint is the lack of skills. Here is Jamie's assessment of the constraints on the architecture:

> We have very little time to get this high-priority project to market. We lack the skills at the current time, and we need to find ways to get to market with less hardware than in the past.

Jamie decides that based on these constraints he needs to evaluate where within the business architecture he can leverage SaaS solutions to address the constraints. He knows from his studies that anything that is not a core competency is a good candidate for leveraging SaaS solutions. After reviewing the business architecture, he writes down the following components as SaaS candidates for his team to research and validate:

API layer. His team has limited experience writing Representational State Transfer (RESTful) APIs in the cloud. They have to support multiple third parties, resulting in the need to support multiple stacks, manage API traffic performance, quickly integrate new partners, and so forth. An API management SaaS tool looks like a good solution.

My cart. There are many shopping cart SaaS solutions available.

Payments. If they offload payments to a Payment Card Industry Data Security Standard (PCI DSS)-certified SaaS solution, the entire platform will not be in scope for PCI DSS audits. This will save a lot of time and money.

Utility services. All of the utility services are candidates for SaaS because they are not core competencies. However, they may be provided from a PaaS or IaaS solution, as well.

Enterprise systems. The ERP, financial system, and CRM systems are perfect candidates for SaaS as they are not core competencies and there is no added business value for managing them internally. They are not in the critical path for the first phase (integrate with third parties), but they may have a significant contribution to the goal of reducing infrastructure.

When to Use PaaS

PaaS is the least mature of the three cloud service models. The first generation of PaaS solutions, like Google, Force.com, and Microsoft Azure, required that the buyers use a specific programming language and run on the service provider's infrastructure. For start-ups and small businesses these constraints may have been acceptable, but for enterprises it is quite a different story. Enterprises are complex organizations with many different architectures, technology stacks, and application needs. The lack of flexibility for both the programming language and the infrastructure turned off many enterprises and slowed the adoption of PaaS. Over the past few years a number of second-generation

PaaS service providers have emerged. These service providers saw an opportunity to address the enterprise customers' needs. Many of these new PaaS vendors now support multiple stacks and some allow the PaaS software to be deployed on the infrastructure of the service consumer's choosing. In addition to the newer PaaS service providers, many of the original PaaS service providers now support multiple languages like Ruby, PHP, Python, and Node.js. Cloud Foundry and OpenShift are two open source projects that are gaining traction and can be deployed on any infrastructure. One of the advantages of open source cloud-based solutions is that with commercial vendors, if they go out of business, the service consumer has no choice but to quickly move to another platform. With open source the service consumers have control over the software and stay on the platform for as long as they wish.

Public PaaS service providers manage the underlying infrastructure, networks, storage devices, and operating systems. Tasks like monthly security patching, logging, monitoring, scaling, fail over, and other system administration-related tasks are provided by the vendor so the developers can focus on building cloud-ready applications.

Private PaaS service providers do not provide the abstraction of the infrastructure services like the public PaaS providers do. Private PaaS offers the capability to deploy the PaaS software on both a private and public cloud (hybrid) but at the sacrifice of requiring the service consumer to manage the application stack and the infrastructure.

PaaS vendors provide a platform that is shared by many customers. In order to manage the performance, reliability, and scalability of each customer and to ensure the heavy loads from one customer do not impact the performance of another customer, the PaaS vendors have various limits that they enforce on developers. These limits, sometimes called *throttling*, protect the platform from getting overloaded by an individual customer, thus protecting all customers in the process. Most PaaS vendors throttle an individual user's bandwidth to protect against network collisions and congestion. Some PaaS vendors throttle CPU utilization to reduce the amount of heat generation in the data center and to conserve power. Other PaaS vendors that price based on fixed amounts of consumption such as blocks of storage will throttle the customer when the customer has consumed all of the resources that they have paid for. Developers must understand the limitations of their selected platform and design accordingly.

Many PaaS service providers protect their platform and its customers by throttling the database activity of customers. Developers must account for this in their designs. One way is to trap for these types of errors and retry until successful. Another method is to break units of work into smaller chunks before calling the database. This trick can be used to design around bandwidth limitations, as well. For some applications, designing around throttles creates unacceptable delays in processing time or it may impact the quality and reliability of the application. If this is the case, then PaaS may not be the right service model and IaaS should be used instead. Websites with extremely high volumes or highly distributed applications that crunch through enormous amounts of data are typically poor candidates for PaaS.

But not every application or service has the extreme processing requirements of a streaming video company like Netflix or a popular social media website like Twitter. Many workflow-driven B2B-type applications are prime candidates for PaaS. In a typical workflow, a product starts with an order and flows through a repeatable process flow until the product is built, sold, shipped, and invoiced. Dell uses Salesforce.com's platform called Force.com to deliver $1 billion in deal registrations with over 100,000 channel partners, so it is safe to say that PaaS solutions can scale admirably.

AEA CASE STUDY: Use Case for PaaS

Now that Jamie has identified which components within the architecture are candidates for SaaS, the remaining components all require development. He now looks at the remaining components to determine which components can leverage a PaaS so that they can get to market quickly without having to manage infrastructure and the application stack. Jamie assessed the current web traffic and predicted future web traffic. Based on these numbers he feels that a PaaS can support their web traffic for the next two years, but by year three the load may be too great. Of course, these are just assumptions because no vendors have been selected yet and this hypothesis would need to be tested. However, Jamie needs to balance the short-term goal of getting to market quickly against the long-term goal of scaling to eBay levels.

Jamie decides to leverage PaaS for seller components because the seller activity drives much less traffic than buyer activity. Sellers create content and manage their inventory, while buyers generate millions of transactions while interacting with auctions and browsing products. Jamie jots down the components that are candidates for PaaS:

Seller services. Lower volume, moderate number of customers.

Mobile touchpoint. The team has very little mobile experience and is required to develop for many different types of phones and tablets. A mobile development platform would accelerate the development process and reduce the amount of overall development.

Social touchpoint. Measuring the impact of the various social touchpoints could be a major project. Leveraging a social marketing platform eliminates a large amount of work and provides the team with deep analytics and campaign management capabilities.

Utility services. The PaaS likely provides services for security, event triggering, notifications, and APIs to connect to the popular social sites. One thing to consider, though, is that the buyer services will be run on an IaaS and will be leveraging utility services provided on the IaaS platform. The team will need to perform some due diligence to determine if they should leverage a single set of utility services from the IaaS vendor or if they can also use the utility services from the PaaS vendor.

Jamie determines that if the PaaS and IaaS utility services are compatible and the user experiences of the buyers and sellers are the same when it comes to security, notifications, social, and so forth, then leveraging both PaaS utility services and IaaS utility services is acceptable. After all, some sellers are also buyers. If, for whatever reason, the differences of the IaaS and PaaS utility services create different user experiences, the applications built on top of PaaS will have to leverage the underlying IaaS APIs. Keep in mind that Jamie has not yet determined if they are using public, private, or hybrid clouds. If they are using public clouds, then this is not an issue because the public PaaS also is responsible for the IaaS layer. If they are using a private PaaS, AEA is responsible for the IaaS layer.

When to Use IaaS

If an application or service has performance or scalability requirements that require the developers to manage memory, configure database servers and application servers to maximize throughput, specify how data is distributed across disk spindles, manipulate the operating system, and so on, then you should leverage IaaS. If you don't need to worry about those things, then you should consider PaaS.

At M-Dot Network we had a requirement to deliver 1 million transactions per minute from retailer POS systems to the cloud and back in subsecond response time. In order to accomplish that feat we could not be throttled by our cloud vendor, and we had to make tweaks to the operating system, the application server, and the database to achieve the desired throughput.

Another factor is cost. PaaS can reduce costs substantially by reducing the amount of work and the number of resources required to build and deploy applications. However, the PaaS pay-as-you-go model can get extremely expensive when data gets into the tens of terabytes or when the bandwidth or CPU demands exceed normal levels. As of March 5, 2013, Amazon has reduced the costs of its EC2 (Elastic Compute Cloud) 26 times, and other IaaS vendors have been following its lead. As time progresses the cost of IaaS may become so low that PaaS providers might have to follow suit in order to compete.

Another reason for leveraging IaaS over PaaS is related to mitigating risks of downtime. When a PaaS provider has an outage, the customer can only wait for the provider to fix the issue and get the services back online. The same is true for SaaS solutions. With IaaS, the customer can architect for failure and build redundant services across multiple physical or virtual data centers. AWS has had some highly publicized outages in recent years and major websites like Reddit, Foursquare, and others were down. But many other sites survived the outage due to cross-zone redundancy. Most times when AWS has an outage, PaaS provider Heroku, which runs its services on top of AWS, is impacted. Heroku customers are out of luck until both AWS and Heroku recover. Many AWS customers can and have survived an AWS outage.

As we move up the stack toward SaaS we increase speed to market, reduce the number of human resources required, and reduce operational costs. As we move down the stack toward IaaS, we get more control of the infrastructure and have a better chance of avoiding or recovering from a vendor outage.

AEA CASE STUDY: Use Case for IaaS

All remaining components are candidates for IaaS. Jamie has determined that the future transaction count is too high for PaaS, and he believes he can still meet the date even though it will take more work leveraging IaaS. Here is his list of components that will run on IaaS.

Buyer services. High volume, millions of customers.

Business process. The workflow will be built on IaaS but will call out to services that handle the payments (SaaS) and pay sellers (integration with bank).

Utility services. Leverage the IaaS utility services.

Common business services. These are high-volume services shared by both the buyers and sellers.

AEA CASE STUDY: Cloud Deployment Models

The next thing for Jamie to research is what cloud deployment model makes sense for AEA. After meeting with the product manager and other business and IT stakeholders, Jamie wrote down the following notes about deployment models:

- PCI DSS is out of scope due to selecting SaaS vendor for payments and leveraging a bank for transferring funds to sellers.

- Limited amount of PII (personal identifiable information) data, and users accept terms and conditions when they register.
- Sellers may be located outside of the United States and have concerns with data in the public cloud.
- Risk of public PaaS and IaaS outages.
- Need to reduce infrastructure footprint.
- Need to get to market fast.

Most of these constraints point to using a public cloud. Since this platform does not require heavy regulation and speed to market is urgent, the public cloud option is very attractive. One concern that Jamie has is the public cloud might scare away international third parties. Another concern Jamie has is how to deal with cloud service provider outages. He knows from his research that if he leverages a public IaaS provider like AWS, he can maintain uptime when AWS has outages, but it requires significant investments in redundancy and fail over. He also knows that if the public PaaS has an outage, he is at the mercy of the provider until it recovers. However, if the PaaS goes down, only the seller services are impacted, not the auctions. The only impact is that new products can't be listed, but sales will be able to continue. Jamie accepts that risk for the time being.

Long term, Jamie decides that a hybrid cloud solution makes the best sense. With a hybrid solution, Jamie can keep all critical data on-premises and attract more international partners. He can have the baseline workloads running on-premises and leverage the public cloud for spikes in traffic. In addition, the public and private cloud can provide fail over for each other. He can leverage a hybrid PaaS that can run on both the private and public cloud.

However, Jamie has a short-term fixed date that is very aggressive. Building private cloud solutions is much more involved than public cloud solutions. It also does not help meet the goal of reducing the infrastructure footprint. Jamie builds a roadmap that shows a public-cloud-only option in the first six months. The public cloud solution will have to include redundancy across virtual data centers. In order to justify adding servers for the private cloud that he targets year two to deliver, he also recommends moving the CRM and ERP systems to SaaS solutions, which will reduce a large amount of infrastructure costs in both hardware and licensing.

Jamie's decisions are unique to his company. His decisions were impacted by the business case, the time constraints, his organization's readiness, and his personal knowledge and experience of his industry and his customers. There are no right or wrong choices here. Jamie could have chosen to do the entire solution in a private cloud or entirely on public PaaS and would likely be successful. But he weighed in on the constraints and made the best decisions he could based on the information he had.

Common Cloud Use Cases

For start-ups and greenfield applications, it is common that entire applications are built in the cloud. For established enterprises, it is more realistic that only certain components within an architecture are deployed in the cloud. Here are some common use cases where today's enterprises are leveraging the cloud to supplement their existing architectures.

Cloud Bursting

Many organizations choose to leverage the cloud to handle peaks in traffic. They may have applications running in their data centers and choose to send excess capacity out to a cloud service provider instead of investing in physical infrastructure to accommodate peaks. Retailers that deal with seasonal spikes around the holidays or companies that process tax returns that have low traffic for most of the year but experience huge peaks during the tax season are examples of companies that might take advantage of cloud bursting.

Archiving/Storage

Some organizations are finding innovative ways to reduce archiving and storage costs by leveraging storage in the cloud. Traditional archiving strategies involve several pieces of infrastructure and software such as backup tape and disk devices, various types of storage media, transportation services, and much more. Now companies can eliminate all of those physical components and leverage cloud storage services that can be totally automated through scripts. The cost of storage in the cloud is drastically cheaper than storage on physical storage media and the processes for data retrieval can be much less complex.

Data Mining and Analytics

The cloud is a great place for processing large amounts of data on-demand. As disks gets cheaper, organizations are storing more data now than ever before. It is not uncommon for companies to be storing many terabytes or even petabytes of information. Analyzing large amounts of data like this can become very challenging on-premises because an extraordinary amount of infrastructure is required to process all of that data. To make matters worse, the analytics of these large data sets are usually ad hoc in nature, which means often the infrastructure is sitting idle until someone initiates a request.

Moving these types of big data workloads to a public cloud is much more economical. In the public cloud, resources can be provisioned only when a request is initiated. There is a huge cost savings both in physical infrastructure and in the management of the systems by deploying an on-demand cloud model.

Test Environments

Many companies are looking to the cloud for provisioning test and development environments and other nonproduction environments. In the past, IT has had to maintain numerous test and development environments on-premises, which required constant patching and maintenance. In many cases, those environments sit idle outside of normal working hours when workers are not working. Another issue is that a limited number of environments are usually available to testers and developers, and they often have to share environments with other teams and environments, which can make testing and development a challenge.

To solve that problem, many companies are creating processes for testers and developers to self-provision testing and development environments on-demand in the cloud. This method requires less work for the administrators, provides speed to market for the testers and developers, and can reduce costs if the environments are shut down when not in use. Better performance testing can be accomplished in the cloud because testers can provision a large amount of resources to simulate large peaks in traffic, where in the on-premises model they were restricted to the amount of physical hardware that was in the data center.

There are many more use cases for cloud computing. The point here is that building services in the cloud is not an all-or-nothing proposition. It is perfectly acceptable and very common for enterprises to have a mixture of solutions within their architectures deployed within their data centers and in one-to-many clouds.

Summary

Choosing cloud service models and deployment models are critical tasks in any cloud computing initiative. The decisions should be based on business drivers, constraints, and customer impacts. Before making these decisions it is highly recommended that the six architecture questions discussed in Chapter 4 are answered. It is also important that all components of the business architecture are considered before making these decisions. An understanding of the future state is also important. As we saw from Jamie's decision, he built a roadmap that arrives at a long-term future state of a hybrid cloud, which is much different from the initial deliverable, which is a public cloud option. Since he knows that his future state is a hybrid cloud solution, he knows that a hybrid PaaS makes sense in his first deliverable. If he did not look out to the future, he likely would have chosen a public PaaS. When the time came to move to a hybrid solution he would have been constrained by the public PaaS decision. The moral of this story is to take time up front to understand the context of the entire business problem over time, not just the immediate need.

References

Kaplan, J. (2005). *Strategic IT Portfolio Management: Governing Enterprise Transformation.* PRTM, Inc.

Handler, R., and B. Maizlish (2005). *IT Portfolio Management: Unlocking the Business Value of Technology.* Hoboken, NJ: John Wiley & Sons.

Hurwitz, J., M. Kaufman, F. Halper, and D. Kirsch (2012). *Hybrid Cloud for Dummies.* Hoboken, NJ: John Wiley & Sons.

Lee, J. (2013, March 5). "Amazon Web Services Drops Prices Again to Compete with Microsoft, Google." Retrieved from http://www.thewhir.com/web-hosting-news/amazon-web-services-drops-price-of-ec2-again-to-compete-with-microsoft-google.

CHAPTER 6

The Key to the Cloud

RESTful Services

> Life is a distributed object system. However, communication among humans is a distributed hypermedia system, where the mind's intellect, voice+gestures, eyes+ears, and imagination are all components.
> —Roy T. Fielding, inventor of REST

There are many reasons that Representational State Transfer (RESTful) services are a critical component of any cloud solution. First, when building services in the cloud one typically builds on top of an Infrastructure as a Service (IaaS) or Platform as a Service (PaaS) provider or integrates with one-to-many Software as a Service (SaaS) offerings. All of these cloud service providers have exposed their application programming interfaces (APIs) using RESTful services. In addition, clouds are heterogeneous ecosystems that connect many different services from many different companies written in many different technology stacks. The complexities of the underlying stacks and protocols should be abstracted away from the business logic so this ecosystem of services can easily connect and work in harmony.

A great example of this concept in practice is how simply we can plug in social media functionality from Facebook, Twitter, Pinterest, and other social media touchpoints. Underneath those widely used APIs are some very diverse and complex systems. These high-scale systems combine multiple programming stacks, multiple database technologies, and technologies for integration, caching, queuing, event processing, and much more. The beauty of services is that all of that complexity is hidden from us as developers and literally within minutes we can connect our applications and services and leverage all of that wonderful, complex functionality with no knowledge of how the underlying technologies work. That is agility at its finest.

A second reason that RESTful services are a critical component of any cloud solution pertains to the many touchpoints that users consume information on in today's day and age. Gone are the days of building separate systems for individual touchpoints. Today, the preferred method is to build multiple user interfaces (web, mobile, tablet, etc.) that leverage the same services and are always in sync. We have to build things this way because our users are bouncing around between devices and browsers and will leave in droves if each touchpoint displays different result sets. To make things even easier, there are a few new companies that are delivering mobile platforms so that developers can build a single user interface (UI), and the platforms will transform the code into the various mobile and tablet user interfaces. Did I mention agility?

Third, and most important, cloud infrastructure is virtual and dynamic, meaning resources come and go in an elastic matter and every piece of cloud infrastructure is expected to fail. The cloud is designed to be fault-tolerant so that if any node fails, the system can continue its operations either in a degraded mode or without any degradation if other nodes become available to replace the failed node. To take advantage of fault-tolerant cloud infrastructure, software must be built to be fault-tolerant as well. To accomplish fault tolerance with software, the software must not be tightly coupled to the infrastructure. A key best practice to writing loosely coupled software in the cloud is to store the application state on the client instead of the server, thus breaking the dependencies between the hardware and the software. This concept is a core principle for building RESTful web services.

This chapter will discuss why REST is so important when building cloud architectures. Migrating legacy applications to the cloud can be a challenge. We will discuss what those challenges are and how to deal with them.

Why REST?

Before going much further, this is a good time to discuss REST in more detail. Dr. Roy Fielding, the creator of the architectural approach called REST, looked at how the Internet, a highly distributed network of independent resources, worked collectively with no knowledge of any resource located on any server. Fielding applied those same concepts to REST by declaring the following four major constraints.

1. **Separation of resource from representation**. Resources and representations must be loosely coupled. For example, a resource may be a data store or a chunk of code, while the representation might be an XML or JSON result set or an HTML page.
2. **Manipulation of resources by representations**. A representation of a resource with any metadata attached provides sufficient information to modify or delete the resource on the server, provided the client has permission to do so.

THE KEY TO THE CLOUD

3. **Self-descriptive messages**. Each message provides enough information to describe how to process the message. For example, the "Accept application/xml" command tells the parser to expect XML as the format of the message.
4. **Hypermedia as the engine of application state (HATEOAS)**. The client interacts with applications only through hypermedia (e.g., hyperlinks). The representations reflect the current state of the hypermedia applications.

Let's look at these constraints one at a time. By separating the resource from its representation, we can scale the different components of a service independently. For example, if the resource is a photo, a video, or some other file, it may be distributed across a content delivery network (CDN), which replicates data across a high-performance distributed network for speed and reliability. The representation of that resource may be an XML message or an HTML page that tells the application what resource to retrieve. The HTML pages may be executed on a web server farm across many servers in multiple zones in Amazon's public cloud—Amazon Web Services (AWS)—even though the resource (let's say it is a video) is hosted by a third-party content delivery network (CDN) vendor like AT&T. This arrangement would not be possible if both the resource and the representation did not adhere to the constraint.

The next constraint, manipulation of resources by representations, basically says that resource data (let's say it is a customer row in a MySQL table) can only be modified or deleted on the database server if the client sending the representation (let's say it is an XML file) has enough information (PUT, POST, DELETE) and has permission to do so (meaning that the user specified in the XML message has the appropriate database permissions). Another way to say that is the representation should have everything it needs to request a change to a resource provider assuming the requester has the appropriate credentials.

The third constraint simply says that the messages must contain information that describes how to parse the data. For example, Twitter has an extensive library of APIs that are free for the public to use. Since the end users are unknown entities to the architects at Twitter, they have to support many different ways for users to retrieve data. They support both XML and JSON as output formats for their services. Consumers of their services must describe in their requests which format their incoming messages are in so that Twitter knows which parser to use to read the incoming messages. Without this constraint, Twitter would have to write a new version of each service for every different format that its users might request. With this constraint in place, Twitter can simply add parsers as needed and can maintain a single version of its services.

The fourth and most important constraint is HATEOAS. This is how RESTful services work without maintaining application state on the server side. By leveraging hypermedia as the engine of application state (HATE-OAS), the application state is represented by a series of links—uniform resource identifiers or URIs—on the client side, much like following the site map of a website by following the URLs. When a resource (i.e., server or connection) fails, the resource that resumes working on the services starts with the URI of the failed resource (the application state) and resumes processing.

A good analogy of HATEOAS is the way a GPS works in a car. Punch in a final destination on the GPS and the application returns a list of directions. You start driving by following these directions. The voice on the GPS tells you to turn when the next instruction is due. Let's say you pull over for lunch and shut off the car. When you resume driving, the remaining directions in the trip list pick right up where they left off. This is exactly how REST works via hypermedia. A node failing is similar to shutting your car off for lunch and another node picking up where the failed node left off is similar to restarting the car and the GPS. Make sense?

Why are the four constraints of REST so important when building solutions in the cloud? The cloud, like the Internet, is a massive network of independent resources that are designed to be fault-tolerant. By following the constraints of REST, the software components that run in the cloud have no dependencies on the underlying infrastructure that may fail at any time. If these four constraints are not followed, it creates limitations on the application's ability to scale and to fail over to the next available resource.

As with any architectural constraint, there are trade-offs. The more abstraction that is built into an architecture, the more flexible and agile the architecture will be, but it comes with a price. Building RESTful services correctly takes more up-front time because building loosely coupled services is a much more involved design process. Another trade-off is performance. Abstraction creates overhead, which can impact performance. There may be some use cases where the performance requirements far exceed the benefits of REST and, for that particular use case, another method may be required. There are other design issues to be aware of that are covered in the next section.

The Challenges of Migrating Legacy Systems to the Cloud

One of the challenges companies have when they decide to port applications from on-premises to the cloud is that many of their legacy systems are reliant on ACID transactions. ACID (atomicity, consistency, isolation, durability) transactions are used to ensure that a transaction is complete and consistent. With ACID transactions, a transaction is not complete until it is committed and the data is up to date. In an on-premises environment where data may be tied to a single partition, forcing consistency is perfectly acceptable and often the preferred method. In the cloud, there is quite a different story.

Cloud architectures rely on Basically Available, Soft State, Eventually Consistent (BASE) transactions. BASE transactions acknowledge that resources can fail and the data will *eventually* become consistent. BASE is often used in volatile environments where nodes may fail or systems need to work whether the user is connected to a network or not. This is extremely important as we move into the world of mobile, where connectivity is spotty at times.

Getting back to the legacy system discussion, legacy systems often rely on ACID transactions, which are designed to run in a single partition and expect the data to be consistent. Cloud-based architectures require partition tolerance, meaning if one instance of a compute resource cannot complete the task, another instance is called on to finish the job. Eventually the discrepancies will be reconciled and life will go on its merry way. However, if a legacy system with ACID transactionality is ported and not modified to deal with partition tolerance, users of the system will not get the data consistency they are accustomed to and they will challenge the quality of the system. Architects will have to account for reconciling inconsistencies, which is nothing new. In retail they call that *balancing the till*, which is an old way of saying making sure the cash in the drawer matches the receipt tape at the end of the day. But many legacy applications were not designed to deal with eventual consistency and will frustrate the end users if they are simply ported to the cloud without addressing this issue.

What about those mega-vendors out there whose legacy applications are now cloud-aware applications? Most of those rebranded dinosaurs are actually running in a single partition and don't really provide the characteristics of cloud-based systems such as rapid elasticity and resource pooling. Instead, many of them are simply large, monolithic legacy systems running on a virtual machine at a hosted facility, a far cry from being a true cloud application. It is critical that architects dig under the covers of these vendor solutions and make sure that they are not being sold snake oil.

There is a new breed of vendors that offer cloud migration services. It is important to note that these solutions are simply porting the legacy architecture as is. What that means is that if the legacy applications can only run in a single tenant, they will not be able to take advantage of the elasticity that the cloud offers. For some applications, there may be no real benefit for porting them to the cloud.

Summary

Architecting solutions for cloud computing requires a solid understanding of how the cloud works. To build resilient solutions that scale, one must design a solution with the expectation that everything can and will fail. Cloud infrastructure is designed for high availability and is partition tolerant in nature. Migrating single-partition applications to the cloud makes the migration act more like a hosting solution rather than a scalable cloud solution. Building stateless, loosely coupled, RESTful services is the secret to thriving in this highly available, eventually consistent world. Architects must embrace this method of building software to take advantage of the elasticity that the cloud provides.

References

Bloomberg, J. (2013). *The Agile Architecture Revolution: How Cloud Computing, REST-Based SOA, and Mobile Computing Are Changing Enterprise IT*. Hoboken, NJ: John Wiley & Sons.

Bloomberg, J. (2011, June 1). "BASE Jumping in the Cloud: Rethink Data Consistency." Retrieved from http://www.zapthink.com/2011/06/01/base-jumping-in-the-cloud-rethinking-data-consistency/.

Fielding, R. (2000). "Representational State Transfer (REST)," in "Architectural Styles and the Design of Network-based Software Architectures." Ph.D. Dissertation, University of California, Irvine. Retrieved from http://www.ics.uci.edu/~fielding/pubs/dissertation/rest_arch_style.htm.

Hoff, T. (2013, May 1). "Myth: Eric Brewer on Why Banks Are BASE Not ACID—Availability Is Revenue." Retrieved from http://highscalability.com/blog/2013/5/1/myth-eric-brewer-on-why-banks-are-base-not-acid-availability.html.

CHAPTER 7

Auditing in the Cloud

Two thirds of the earth's surface is covered with water, the other third is covered with auditors from headquarters.
                                              —NORMAN R. AUGUSTINE

Historically, data has been stored behind corporate firewalls in the control of the company that owns the data. It was up to the company to secure the perimeter, harden the infrastructure, and secure the databases. Auditors could come on-site and inspect the processes and controls to make their assessments. If any government agency wanted to seize any data for an investigation, it had to confront the company before doing so. The bottom line was the company that owned the data was in control. That is not the same as saying the data was secure, but responsibility for securing the data was owned by the company.

Storing the data in the cloud is a different story. Now the company has a shared responsibility with the cloud service provider (CSP) and the further up the cloud stack they go, the more responsibility the CSP takes on. In some respects this is a good thing. Why not let the CSP, whose core competencies include security and compliance, handle some of the heavy lifting around securing and encrypting data, hardening the environment, managing backup and recovery processes, and various other infrastructure-related tasks? Off-loading security and compliance to a CSP does not mean that the company is no longer accountable. It simply means the CSP provides secure and compliant cloud services, but it is still up to the company to secure the overall application. When security and compliance are shared responsibilities, auditing the entire solution becomes a more complex situation. Now auditing must occur across multiple entities: cloud service consumer and cloud services provider(s).

This chapter will discuss the cloud security, what auditors look for in cloud applications, briefly review common regulations, and then cover various design strategies for auditing cloud services.

Data and Cloud Security

Study after study and poll after poll consistently point to security in the cloud as the number-one concern of both business and IT people. Some of these concerns are valid but some are based on assumptions and fear. IT people are used to being in control of their data and systems. Letting someone else manage critical data is a foreign concept to many, and the immediate reaction is to assume that if it is out of our control, it cannot be as secure. A recent study by Alert Logic in the spring of 2013 came to the following conclusions.

- The cloud is *not* inherently less safe than enterprise data centers.
- Attacks in CSP environments tend to be crimes of opportunity, while those in enterprise data centers tend to be more targeted and sophisticated.
- Web applications are equally threatened in cloud and enterprise data centers.

What this means is that it doesn't matter where the data resides—the threats are the same. What was more interesting in the study was that the success rate of penetrations from outside threats was much higher in enterprise data centers than in CSP environments. This should not be much of a surprise since security is a core competency of CSPs. Without world-class security, many would not be in business today. Many corporations do not have the resources and expertise to build a world-class secure data center.

Based on this information, skeptical architects and product managers need to dismiss the notion that data cannot be secure in the cloud and focus on the real issues and constraints around auditing, laws and compliance issues, customer requirements, and risks.

Auditing Cloud Applications

Auditors are responsible for validating that their clients adequately address a collection of controls and processes in order to receive a stamp of approval for satisfying the requirements of a given set of constraints as defined by a governing set of laws. There are many different regulations that exist today. In order for a company to determine which regulations apply to it, the company must have a firm understanding of its industry's standards, business processes, and data requirements. When dealing with IT systems, auditors validate the process and controls in the following areas (when necessary):

- **Physical environment.** Perimeter security, data center controls, and so on.

- **Systems and applications.** Security and controls of network, databases, software, and the like.
- **Software development life cycle (SDLC).** Deployments, change management, and so forth.
- **Personnel.** Background checks, drug testing, security clearance, and more.

Before cloud computing, an auditor could sit down with a client and map personnel and physical infrastructure to the different controls and processes that were to be audited. Auditors had access to physical data centers whether they were located at a client's property or at a third-party facility. In either case, the auditors could point to a physical machine and inspect the physical security of the data center. In the cloud, this is not the case. Now, certain controls and processes map to a CSP instead of to an individual. When that occurs, the auditor must rely on the auditing information produced by that CSP, hence the reason why compliance is such a high priority in the cloud. Without proof of compliance, a CSP could cause a customer to fail its audit. This is one major reason why some companies prefer to build private clouds. They want to be in total control of the data, the processes, and the controls and not rely on another entity when it comes to security, privacy, and regulation. The irony of that decision is that in many cases, it would be easier and more cost effective to rely on CSPs if certain functions of the application were managed by certified CSPs.

A public Infrastructure as a Service (IaaS) environment is a multitenant environment, meaning multiple customers share compute resources. The IaaS provider will not allow an auditor of one of its tenants to access the infrastructure because it has an obligation to protect the rights of all of the other tenants. The IaaS provider will have its own auditors audit its perimeter security, processes, and controls, but no tenant's auditor will be able to physically access the actual infrastructure (the tenant has no idea what infrastructure it is running on, anyway). Auditors will be forced to inspect the white papers and published audit reports that the IaaS providers produce and will have no access to public IaaS data centers. For private IaaS data centers, auditors may have access to inspect the actual infrastructure to access the physical perimeter security unless the private cloud is hosted by a CSP.

With Platform as a Service (PaaS) CSPs, the physical aspects of auditing are even more complex. Not only is the infrastructure abstracted and managed by the CSP, the application stack is, too. Tasks like monthly patching, locking down the operating system, intrusion detecting, and others are all managed by the CSP. In some instances, even the database is controlled and managed by the CSP, and the customer only controls the database access and administration of users. Even more responsibility is outsourced to the CSP with Software as a

Service (SaaS) applications. In addition to being responsible for the infrastructure and application stack, SaaS providers also have responsibility for the entire application. Consumers of SaaS solutions have very limited responsibilities in this case. In Chapter 9, "Security Design in the Cloud," we will discuss this in great detail.

Why is all of this important? There are a number of regulations that must be adhered to if a company wishes to operate certain business processes in the cloud. Many customers will not do business with a company that offers cloud services that are not in compliance with various regulations. For example, a U.S.-based company offering cloud-based services for automating health records processing on behalf of health care providers will have a very hard time finding a customer if it is not HIPAA compliant. HIPAA is the Health Insurance Portability and Accountability Act put in place by the United States federal government that requires health care providers to apply appropriate levels of administrative, technical, and physical controls to ensure the privacy of consumers' protected health information (PHI). Health care providers are very unlikely to engage with a CSP that is not HIPAA compliant because by doing so, the health care provider may fall out of compliance, which could lead to unpleasant consequences for its business, such as fines, legal issues, lost business, and bad publicity.

It is important that architects and product managers understand who is responsible for the data within each service model and how that responsibility is accessed in the audit process so the appropriate processes and controls can be put in place. It is equally important to understand when certain regulatory requirements are in scope, which leads us to our next section.

Regulations in the Cloud

There are a number of regulations that apply to systems being built in the cloud. Some are industry specific, some are specific to the type of data and transactions that are being processed, and others are standards for any cloud-based system. For companies building software in the cloud, there are two parties that have a responsibility to adhere to compliance: the CSP and the company building the applications. The fact that a company like Amazon Web Services (AWS) is certified for the ISO 27001 standard does not make the applications built on top of AWS compliant. It simply means the infrastructure layer can pass the audit. The company building and managing the application stack and application layer has to have all of the proper controls in place to ensure that the entire application can pass the audit. Table 7.1 offers a list of some of the regulations that can come into play when building cloud services.

Table 7.1   Regulations and Controls

Audit	Category	Description
ISO27001	Software	International standards for computer system
SSAE-16	Security	Controls for finance, security, and privacy
Directive 95/46/ec	Security	European security and privacy controls
Directive 2002/58/ec	Security	European e-privacy controls
SOX	Financial	U.S. public company financial accountability controls
PCI DSS	Credit Card	Security and privacy of credit card information
HIPAA	Health	Security and privacy of health care information
FedRAMP	Security	U.S. government security standards for cloud computing
FIPS	Software	U.S. government standard for computer systems
FERPA	Education	Security and privacy of education information

To pass audits pertaining to software best practices, security, and privacy, a company must have controls and processes in place in the following categories:

- Incident management
- Change management
- Release management
- Configuration management
- Service level agreements
- Availability management
- Capacity planning
- Business continuity
- Disaster recovery
- Access management
- Governance
- Data management
- Security management

This is another reason the myth that cloud solutions are not secure is completely false. In order to become certified for the standard regulations for cloud computing, a company must pass audits by implementing approved processes and controls in all of these categories. Many on-premises solutions were never held to that same standard. We will discuss some of these categories in detail later in the book.

There are many more regulations that can fall into scope. Each country may have its own laws that must be adhered to, as well. The type of application and the customer base have a lot to do with the regulations that apply. For example, many social media sites do not feel the need to invest in passing various audits. Most simply post terms and conditions of what the company's responsibilities are and the user accepts them as is in return for using the services. For business-to-business (B2B) companies, adherence to regulations is much stricter. Customers of CSPs that are corporations have much greater responsibility and requirements than individual consumers. For example, an individual using a cloud service like Twitter can choose to opt in and assume the risks as defined in the terms of services or she can choose to not enroll. If an individual opts in, she relies on Twitter to uphold its part of the agreement by keeping her data secure and private. If Twitter fails to do so, there is not much an individual can do other than choose to close her account.

Now let's look at Chatter, a Twitter-like cloud service for social collaboration within the enterprise. Even though Twitter and Chatter are conceptually very similar services, the risk of a breach of Chatter data is exponentially more serious than Twitter data. The reason is because Chatter is used internally for business discussions and to connect with customers and suppliers. The information shared using this technology is not for public knowledge. A breach could expose a company's secrets, upset customers and partners, and create a public relations nightmare for the company. Salesforce.com, the company that sells Chatter services, must comply with numerous regulations in order to gain the confidence of businesses if they are to become paying customers.

Here is what decision makers need to know when it comes to regulations. For Infrastructure as a Service (IaaS) and PaaS CSPs, gaining certifications for numerous regulations is a key to customer acquisition. Minimally, a CSP should be certified in ISO 27001 and SSAE-16 SOC1 and SOC2. If the provider expects to have health care customers, it should get certified in HIPAA. PCI compliance is critical if the CSP expects any type of application that accepts payments to be run on its infrastructure. There are a variety of government regulations like Federal Information Processing Standards (FIPS) and the Federal Risk and Authorization Management Program (FedRAMP) in the United States that certain government agencies require CSPs to comply with. Often, companies and government agencies leverage private cloud IaaS and PaaS solutions to get around the lack of certifications in the public cloud space. In these cases, the risks far outweigh the benefits of elasticity and resource pooling that are sacrificed when cloud services are performed in a private cloud setting. Recently, public IaaS providers have been getting certified in federal regulations in an attempt to attract business from government agencies. AWS has launched a dedicated region called GovCloud that meets the regulatory requirements of the government and isolates the government applications installed in that region from the rest of AWS's customers. This is a semiprivate community cloud running on a public IaaS only for certain government agencies.

For SaaS CSPs, privacy is a key issue because all of the data management is the responsibility of the service provider. Most SaaS contracts have a software escrow provision to account for what happens to the data if the solution is unavailable for a long period of time or if the company goes out of business. The software is deposited in a third-party agent's escrow account and turned over to the consumer of the SaaS solution if the CSP declares bankruptcy or fails to meet the contractual obligations. CSPs that transfer data across international boundaries must meet the regulatory requirements of the safe harbor law. EU safe harbor law prohibits the transfer of personal information to and from European Union (EU) countries to non-European companies that do not meet the EU standards for privacy. Any SaaS provider hoping to sell to EU countries or customers that integrate with EU customers will have to adhere to EU regulations as well as many of the regulations just listed. The good news is that there is a great deal of overlap in these regulations. The combination of ISO 27001 and PCI regulations are a superset of a majority of the remaining regulatory requirements. Some auditors even have the capability to combine the auditing efforts into a single engagement so that they can audit all of the processes and controls in one pass and produce multiple audit reports, thus reducing the overall cost and time to complete the audits.

Audit Design Strategies

The first step of an audit design strategy for a new cloud application is to identify all of the regulations that apply based on the requirements from customers and the industry. Most cloud services targeting business customers will be required to be compliant with an IT best practices regulation like the ISO 27001 standard and a security regulation such as the SSAE-16, SOC 2 regulation. Other factors that dictate additional regulations are:

- Industry requirements (health care, government, education, etc.)
- Data types (payments, personal identifiable information, etc.)
- Location (country, transmission across country boundaries, etc.)

Once the team has established the list of regulations that it must adhere to, the next step is to create a work stream in the product roadmap dedicated to auditing. This work stream should be made up of the following strategies:

- Data management (Chapter 8)
- Security management (Chapter 9)

- Centralized logging (Chapter 10)
- SLA management (Chapter 11)
- Monitoring (Chapter 12)
- Disaster recovery (Chapter 13)
- SDLC and automation (Chapter 14)
- Operations and support (Chapter 14)
- Organizational change management (Chapter 15)

A key takeaway here is that the product has to evolve over time. There is much to do within each strategy before attempting to pass an audit. A wise strategy would be to take an enterprise view for each of these strategies, so subsequent applications can leverage the initial investment, and future cloud applications can be implemented in a consistent manner reducing maintenance costs and improving auditability. Addressing auditing requirements after applications are built is a very expensive undertaking and often results in process and control gaps. When auditing requirements are considered early in the development, processes and controls can be designed to be part of the core application, thus making reducing risks, improving auditability, and reducing auditing costs easier.

The amount of development required to build a system that can pass audits is greatly impacted by the cloud service model that a cloud service consumer chooses. When building on top of IaaS, a large amount of the responsibility falls on the cloud service consumer. If the consumer chooses to build its own private cloud on its own premises, the consumer has total responsibility to build in all of the necessary processes and controls. Leveraging a public IaaS or a hosted private IaaS provider off-loads the responsibility for the infrastructure layer to the CSP. Obviously, as we move up the stack to PaaS and SaaS, more responsibility shifts to the CSPs, but the consumer still needs some level of process and controls in each area.

Another key factor of an auditing strategy is the maturity of the consumer. If the consumer is a start-up, it is likely that getting to market quickly is far more important than passing audits. In fact, there is no use putting all of the effort into auditing until the start-up can validate that there is a sufficient demand for its products and services. That is not to say that start-ups should ignore auditing requirements altogether. They should be able to at least answer to customers regarding how they plan on addressing auditing requirements. A well-established company that sells into fortune 500 companies will likely be required to pass the audits prior to launching its products and services.

One of the best examples of implementing an auditing and compliance roadmap is Amazon and its AWS product. Amazon first launched its S3 and EC2 web services to the public in 2006. It wasn't until 2010 that AWS announced it was compliant with ISO 27001 and PCI DSS. In 2011, it announced the publication of the SSAE-16 SOC 1 report. In 2013, it published the SSAE-16

SOC 2 and SOC 3 reports and achieved FedRAMP compliance. This compliance roadmap was driven by customer demand. When AWS first launched and for the following two to three years, it was primarily used by start-ups, web applications, and for ad hoc applications. In order to attract more mainstream customers, Amazon targeted the ISO 27001 standard. Once it was certified for ISO 27001, the feedback the company received was that security in the cloud was a major concern and processing credit card transactions in the cloud was perceived as impossible due to the lack of AWS's PCI DSS certification. Amazon addressed those gaps and then saw huge opportunities to work with the government. The big showstopper for the government projects was the lack of government-related certifications for regulations like FIPS and FedRAMP. Amazon lets the customer demand drive its investments in auditing and compliance.

Summary

There are many regulations and laws that architects and product owners must be aware of before building cloud-based solutions. Knowing the audit requirements up front allows the product team to prioritize tasks along the roadmap so that security, privacy, and other regulatory requirements can be built into the system early on instead of bolted on at the tail end. Awareness of these requirements should create the awareness of the need to design strategies around security, logging, monitoring, SLA management, disaster recovery, and other critical components of a compliant cloud service.

References

Alert Logic, Inc. (2013). "Targeted Attacks and Opportunistic Hacks." State of Cloud Security Report. Spring 2003. Houston.

Aws.amazon.com (2010, December). "December 2010: PCI Compliance and ISO 27001 Certification, Amazon Route 53, Free EC2 Monitoring, GPU Clusters, and More." Retrieved from http://aws.amazon.com/about-aws/newsletters/2010/12/15/december-2010---pci-compliance-and-iso27001-certification/.

AWS.amazon.com (2013). "AWS Achieves FedRAMP Compliance." Retrieved from http://aws.amazon.com/about-aws/whats-new/2013/05/20/aws-achieves-fedramp-compliance/.

Carsaretto, J. (2013, May 17). "Amazon Web Services and Compliance Conversation; SOC 3 Reports Arrive." Retrieved from http://siliconangle.com/blog/2013/05/17/amazon-web-services-starts-the-security-and-compliance-conversation-soc-3-reports-arrive/.

Clark, J. (2012, June 7). "How Amazon Exposed Its Guts: The History of AWS's EC2." Retrieved from http://www.zdnet.com/how-amazon-exposed-its-guts-the-history-of-awss-ec2-3040155310/.

CHAPTER 8

Data Considerations in the Cloud

If we have data, let's look at the data. If we have opinions, let's go with mine.

—Jim Barksdale, former CEO of Netscape

When it comes to cloud computing decision making, nothing influences those decisions more than data requirements. Architects and product managers should have a firm understanding of the requirements for all information that flows in and out of the system. This chapter analyzes the many characteristics of data and how those characteristics influence design decisions.

Data Characteristics

There are many characteristics of data that should be taken into consideration when building cloud services. Here is a short list of categories:

- Physical characteristics
- Performance requirements
- Volatility
- Volume
- Regulatory requirements
- Transaction boundaries
- Retention period

All of the data requirements listed here factor into the decision of how to store the underlying data. There are two key decisions to make that we will discuss toward the end of the chapter:

1. Multitenant or single tenant.
2. Which type of data store to use: SQL, NoSQL, file, and so on.

In the following sections we will discuss design considerations for each data characteristic.

Physical Characteristics

When analyzing physical characteristics, many data points need to be collected. The location of the data is an important piece of information. Does the data already exist or is this a new data set? If it already exists, does the data need to be moved to the cloud or will the data be created in the cloud? If the data has to be transported to the cloud, how big is it? If we are talking about a huge amount of data (terabytes), this presents a challenge. Some cloud vendors offer the capability to ship large amounts of data to them so they can manually load the data on the customer's behalf, but if the data is highly sensitive, do we really want a truckload of sensitive data going off-site? If the data is new, more than likely all of the data can be created in the cloud (public or private) and the ugly step of transferring huge amounts of data for an initial load is not needed. The location of the data also is relevant when analyzing legal responsibilities. Different countries have different laws about data entering and leaving the country's borders.

Who owns the data? Does the company building the software own it, is the data coming from a third party, or does the customer of the system own the data? Can the data be shared with other companies? If so, do certain attributes need to be masked to hide it from other parties? Ownership of data is an important characteristic and the answer to the ownership question should be written in the contracts between the service providers and their customers. For a company building Software as a Service (SaaS), Platform as a Service (PaaS), or Infrastructure as a Service (IaaS) solutions, answers to data ownership and sharing could drive design decisions on whether separate databases and even separate database servers are required per client in order to meet certain demands around privacy, security, and service level agreements (SLAs).

Performance Requirements

Performance falls into three categories: real time, near real time, and delayed time. Real-time performance is usually defined as subsecond response time. Websites typically strive for half-second response time or less. Near real time usually refers to within a second or two. Sometimes near real time means "perceived real time." Perceived real time means the performance is near real time but to the end user it appears to be real time. For example, with point-of-sale (POS) technology, the perceived time for cashing out a customer at the cash register is the time it takes to spit out the receipt after all the items are scanned and the discounts are processed. Often, tasks are performed during the entire shopping experience that may take one second or more, but these tasks are finished by checkout. Even though some tasks take longer than the real-time standard of half a second, the tasks visible to the consumer (generating the receipt) occur in real time, hence the term *perceived* real time. Delayed time can range from a few seconds to batch time frames of daily, weekly, monthly, and so on.

The response time categories drive major design decisions. The faster the response time required, the more likely the architects will need to leverage memory over disk. Common design patterns for high-volume fast-performing data sets are:

- Use a caching layer.
- Reduce the size of data sets (store hash values or binary representations of attributes).
- Separate databases into read-only and write-only nodes.
- Shard data into customer-, time-, or domain-specific shards.
- Archive aging data to reduce table sizes.
- Denormalize data sets.

There are many other methods. Understanding performance requirements is key in driving these types of design decisions.

Volatility

Volatility refers to the frequency in which the data changes. Data sets are either static or dynamic. Static data sets are usually event-driven data that occur in chronological order. Examples are web logs, transactions, and collection data. Common types of information in web logs are page views, referring traffic, search terms, user IP addresses, and the like. Common transactions are bank debits and credits, point-of-sale purchases, stock trading, and so forth. Examples of collection data are readings from manufacturing machines, environmental readings like weather, and human genome data. Static data sets like these are write-once, read-many type data sets because they occur in a point of time but are analyzed over and over to detect patterns and observe behaviors. These data sets often are stored over long periods of time and consume terabytes of data. Large, static data sets of this nature often require nonstandard database practices to maximize performance. Common practices for mining these types of data sets are to denormalize the data, leverage star or snowflake schemas, leverage NoSQL databases, and, more recently, apply big data technologies.

Dynamic data requires entirely different designs. If data is changing frequently, a normalized relational database management system (RDMS) is the most common solution. Relational databases are great for processing ACID (atomicity, consistency, isolation, durability) transactions to ensure the reliability of the data. Normalized relational databases protect the integrity of the data by ensuring that duplicate data and orphan records do not exist.

Another important characteristic of volatility is the *frequency* of the data. One million rows of data a month is a much easier problem to design for than one million rows a minute. The speed at which data flows (add, change, delete) is a huge factor in the overall architecture of the data layer within the cloud. Understanding the different disk storage systems within the cloud is critical. For example, on Amazon Web Services (AWS), S3 is a highly reliable disk storage system, but it is not the highest performing. EBS volumes are local disk systems that lack the reliability and redundancy of S3 but perform faster. It is key to know the data requirements so that the best disk storage system is selected to solve specific problems.

Volume

Volume refers to the amount of data that a system must maintain and process. There are many advantages of using relational databases, but when data volumes hit a certain size, relational databases can become too slow and too expensive to maintain. Architects must also determine how much data is relevant enough to be maintained online and available for access and how much data should be archived or stored on slower and less expensive disks. Volume also impacts the design of a backup strategy. Backing up databases and file systems is a critical component of business continuity and disaster recovery, and it must be compliant with regulations such as SSAE16 and others. Backups tend to consume large amounts of CPU cycles and could impact the overall system performance without a sound design. Full backups are often performed daily while incremental backups are performed multiple times throughout the day. One common strategy is to perform backups on a slave database so that the application performance is not impacted.

Regulatory Requirements

Regulation plays a major role in design decisions pertaining to data. Almost any company delivering cloud services in a B2B model can expect customers to demand certifications in various regulations such as SAS 70, SSAE 16, ISO 27001, HIPAA, PCI, and others. Data that is classified as PII (personally identifiable information) must be encrypted in flight and at rest, which creates performance overhead, especially if those fields have high volatility and volumes. PII data is a big contributor for companies choosing to leverage private and hybrid clouds. Many companies refuse to put sensitive and private data in a public, multitenant environment. Understanding regulatory constraints and risks can drive deployment model decisions.

Transaction Boundaries

Transaction boundaries can be thought of as a unit of work. In e-commerce, shoppers interact with data on a web form and make various changes to the data as they think through their shopping event. When they place an order, all of the decisions they have made are either committed or rejected based on whether they have a valid credit card and available balance or if the items are still in stock. A good example of a transaction boundary is the following process flow common to travel sites like Expedia.com.

A consumer from Chicago is looking to take a family vacation to Disney World in Orlando, Florida. She logs onto Expedia.com and proceeds to book a flight, a hotel, and a rental car. Behind the scenes, Expedia is calling application programming interfaces (APIs) to three different companies, like US Airways for the airfare, Marriott for the hotel, and Hertz for the rental car. As the consumer is guided through the process flow of selecting an airline, a hotel, and a car, the data is uncommitted until the consumer confirms the purchase. Once the consumer confirms the itinerary, Expedia calls the three different vendors' APIs with a request to book the reservation. If any one of the three calls fails, Expedia needs to ask the consumer if she still wants to proceed with the other two. Even though the initial call to US Airways may have been valid, the entire transaction boundary is not yet complete, and, therefore, the flight should not yet be booked. Committing each part of the transaction independently could create real data quality and customer satisfaction issues if any of the parts of the transaction are purchased while other parts fail. The consumer may not want the trip if any one of the three parts of the trip can't be booked.

Understanding transaction boundaries is critical for determining which data points need to store state and which don't. Remember that RESTful (Representational State Transfer) services are stateless by design, so the architect needs to determine the best way to maintain state for this multipart transaction, which might require caching, writing to a queue, writing to a temp table or disk, or some other method. The frequency in which a multipart transaction like the Expedia example occurs and the volume of these transactions also come into play. If this use case is expected to occur often, then writing the data to tables or disk will likely create performance bottlenecks, and caching the data in memory might be a better solution.

Retention Period

Retention period refers to how long data must be kept. For example, financial data is usually required to be stored for seven years for auditing purposes. This does not mean that seven years must be available online; it simply means the data should not be destroyed until it is older than seven years. For example, online banking usually provides six months' to a year's worth of bank statements online. Users need to submit requests for any statements older than a year. These requests are handled in batch and sometimes come with a processing fee, because the bank has to retrieve the data from off-line storage.

Understanding retention periods is a deciding factor in selecting the proper storage solutions. Data that needs to be maintained but does not have to be available online in real time or near real time can be stored on very cheap off-line disk and/or tape solutions. Often this archived data is kept off-site at a disaster recovery site. Data that needs to be retrieved instantly needs to be stored on a fast-performing disk that is redundant and can recover quickly from failures.

Multitenant or Single Tenant

The tenancy of a system should be determined by the data characteristics just described. When referring to the data layer of an architecture, *multitenancy* means that multiple organizations or customers (tenants) share a group of servers. Most definitions would say a single server, but it typically requires multiple servers (i.e., master–slave) to support a tenant. *Single tenant* means that only one tenant is supported per each group of servers. Figures 8.1 and 8.2 show three multitenancy design strategies that each solve a unique set of requirements.

Multitenancy Isolation Approaches

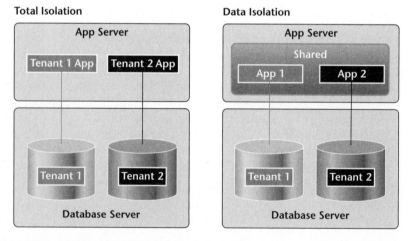

Figure 8.1 Total Isolation and Data Isolation

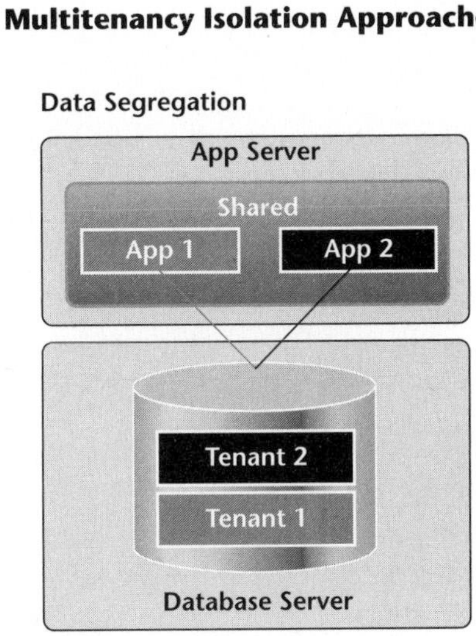

Multitenancy Isolation Approaches

Data Segregation

Figure 8.2   Data Segregation

In Figure 8.1, the image on the left is the "total isolation" strategy, which is an example of single tenant. In this example, both the database layer and the application layer have dedicated resources for each tenant.

Advantages	Disadvantages
Provides independence	Most expensive
Privacy	Minimal reuse
Highest scalability	Highest complexity

By isolating tenants to their own servers, each tenant has a high degree of independence, meaning that if there is an application or database bottleneck in any of the servers, it has limited or no impact on the other tenants. Because no other tenant has access to these servers, there is a higher degree of privacy. Also, systems with dedicated servers for each tenant scale better because of the increase in compute power. However, these advantages come with costs. Single tenant is the most expensive strategy. Each tenant bears an independent cost to the overall system. The ability to reuse existing infrastructure is limited, which creates complexities for managing infrastructure due to the increasing number of servers. The applications must also be infrastructure aware and know how to point to the correct infrastructure.

The image on the right in Figure 8.1 is the "data isolation" strategy. In this model, the application takes a multitenant approach to the application layer by sharing application servers, web servers, and so on. The database layer is single tenant, making this a hybrid approach between multitenancy and single tenant. In this model, we still get the advantages of independence and privacy while reducing some of the cost and complexities. Figure 8.2 shows a true multitenancy model.

The "data segregation" strategy separates the tenants into different database schemas, but they do share the same servers. In this model, all layers are shared for all tenants.

Advantages	Disadvantages
Most cost effective	Lack of independence
Least complex	Lowest performance
Highest reuse	Lowest scalability

This model is the most cost effective due to the large amount of reuse. It is also the least complex because it requires many fewer servers. The challenge is that a performance issue with one tenant can create issues for other tenants. Also, fewer servers means less performance and less scalability. In fact, as tenants are added to the system, the system becomes more vulnerable to failure.

When would we use these strategies? The total isolation approach is commonly used when a tenant has enormous amounts of traffic. In this case it makes sense to dedicate servers to this tenant so it can maximize scaling while not causing disruptions to other clients. The data isolation strategy is often used to protect the privacy of each tenant's data and also to allow tenants to scale independently. The data isolation strategy is often used when the amount of traffic is not overwhelming, yet there still is a need to store a tenant's data in its own schema for privacy reasons.

One company I worked for had many retail clients. Some clients had hundreds and even thousands of stores with several millions shoppers, while other retailers may have had a dozen or fewer stores with shopper counts under a million. The really big retailers were very strict about security and privacy while the smaller chains were not as strict. As a young start-up, we had to balance our costs with our contractual agreements with the retailers. We implemented a hybrid solution. We had one extremely large client that had several thousand stores. We decided to implement a total isolation strategy for this client because of its potential to drive enormous amounts of traffic and because of the importance of delivering to a customer of that size. For all of the smaller retailers that had very average traffic, we used the data segregation model to keep our costs to a minimum. For all other customers that were large to average size in terms of both stores and traffic, we used the data isolation method. Each tenant had its own independent database servers but a shared web and application layer.

Every business is different. It is important to understand what the different tenancy options are. Based on the business requirements, choose the right strategy or combination of strategies to support the needs around independence, security, privacy, scalability, complexity, and costs.

Choosing Data Store Types

Another important design decision to make is what type of data store to use. Many IT shops are very familiar with relational databases and immediately default to solving every data problem with a relational database. You can build a house with a hammer, but if a nail gun is available, you should probably use it.

Relational databases are great for online transaction processing (OLTP) activities because they guarantee that transactions are processed successfully in order for the data to get stored in the database. In addition, relational databases have superior security features and a powerful querying engine. Over the last several years, NoSQL databases have soared in popularity mainly due to two reasons: the increasing amount of data being stored and access to elastic cloud computing resources. Disk solutions have become much cheaper and faster, which has led to companies storing more data than ever before. It is not uncommon for a company to have petabytes of data in this day and age. Normally, large amounts of data like this are used to perform analytics, data mining, pattern recognition, machine learning, and other tasks. Companies can leverage the cloud to provision many servers to distribute workloads across many nodes to speed up the analysis and then deprovision all of the servers when the analysis is finished.

When data gets this big, relational databases just cannot perform fast enough. Relational databases were built to force referential integrity. To accomplish this, a lot of overhead is built into the database engine to ensure that transactions complete and are committed before data is stored into the tables. Relational databases also require indexes to assist in retrieval of records. Once record counts get big enough, the indexes become counterproductive and database performance becomes unacceptable.

NoSQL databases were built to solve these problems. There are four types of NoSQL databases.

Key-Value Store

Key-value store databases leverage a hash table where a unique key with a pointer points to a particular item of the data. This is the simplest of the four NoSQL database types. It is fast and highly scalable and useful for processing massive amounts of writes like tweets. It is also good for reading large, static, structured data like historical orders, events, and transactions. Its disadvantage is that it has no schema, making it a bad choice for handling complex data and relationships. Examples of key-value store databases are Redis, Voldemort (used by LinkedIn), and Amazon's DynamoDB.

Column Store

Column store databases were created to store and process large amounts of data distributed over many machines. The hash key points to multiple columns that are organized in column families. The power of this database is that columns can be added on the fly and do not have to exist in every row. The advantage of column store databases is that they are incredibly fast and scalable and easy to alter on the fly. It is a great database to use when integrating data feeds from different sources with different structures. It is not good for interconnected data sources. Examples of column store databases are Hadoop and Cassandra.

Document Store

Document store databases are used for storing unstructured data stored within documents. Data is often encapsulated with XML, JSON, PDF, Word, Excel, and other common document types. Most logging solutions use a document store to combine log files from many different sources, such as database logs, web server logs, applications server logs, application logs, and so on. These databases are great at scaling large amounts of data made up of different formats but struggle with interconnected data. Examples of document store databases are CouchDB and MongoDB.

Graph Database

Graph databases are used for storing and managing interconnected relationships. These databases are often used to show visual representations of relationships, especially in the area of social media analysis. These databases are great at graphing, but not efficient for much else as the entire relationship tree must be traversed in order to produce results. Examples of graph databases are Neo4j and InfoGrid.

Other Storage Options

We discussed SQL and NoSQL options, but there are also good reasons to store data as files, as well. For example, large files such as photos, videos, and MP3s can be several megabytes or bigger. Web applications that try to store and retrieve these large fields from databases will struggle to create a fast-performing user experience. A better strategy is to leverage a *content delivery network* (CDN). A CDN is a network of distributed computers located in multiple data centers across the Internet that provides high availability and high performance. CDNs are the tool of choice for streaming media and other bandwidth-intensive data.

AEA CASE STUDY: **Data Design Decisions**

After Jamie researched the different data stores he went back to his business architecture diagram to evaluate each component of the architecture. He categorizes his data into the following buckets:

- Online transaction processing (OLTP) data
- Transactional data
- Logging data
- Rich media content
- Financial data

The OLTP data is derived from any of the data entry type activities: customer registrations, content creation, campaign and advertising setups, and so forth. The transactional data refers to the activities that occur during the auction process, such as bids, social interactions, and clicks. Logging data is generated from every component from the applications layer, application stack layer, and infrastructure layer. The rich media content is the videos, images, audio files, and various document files that are uploaded to the system. Last but not least is the financial data, which represents the actual financial transactions (online payments, returns, seller fees).

Jamie reaches the following conclusions that he will present to his team for further vetting:

- **OLTP data**. Relational database
- **Transaction**. NoSQL, column store
- **Logging**. Document store
- **Rich media**. Files, leverage CDN
- **Financial data**. Relational database

He chose a relational database for the OLTP data because the data was being entered in real time online, he wanted to enforce referential data, and he wanted to provide querying capabilities. He chose it for the financial integrity and for its strong security features. He chose a column store database for two reasons. First, he anticipates enormous volumes since he has to record every click and bid that occurs for every auction. Second, because they are integrating with numerous third parties, they anticipate slightly different data formats, which the column store databases are good at handling. The logging will be handled through a logging service either installed on IaaS or provided by a SaaS solution. More than likely the logging tool will leverage a document store. The CDN will be leveraged to optimize performance of the larger files. As the project progresses, Jamie will discover he needs other data stores for things like search and cache. In both cases he will likely leverage either a SaaS solution or a PaaS plug-in, or he will install a solution on top of the IaaS solution.

Summary

There are many characteristics of data, and understanding the characteristics and the requirements for each characteristic is crucial for selecting the correct cloud service model, cloud deployment model, database design(s), and data storage systems. Nobody would ever attempt to build a house without first understanding the requirements of the house and analyzing the floor plan, yet some companies rush to start building software before completely understanding their data requirements. Whether an architect is building a new system or migrating an existing one, the architect would be wise to spend time with the product team to evaluate each of the data characteristics described in this chapter. Without a complete understanding of each data characteristic, it will be extremely difficult to build a system optimized to meet the needs of the business.

Reference

Valentine, D. (2013, February 28). "Rules of Engagement: NoSQL Column Data Stores." Retrieved from http://www.ingenioussql.com/2013/02/28/rules-of-engagement-nosql-column-data-stores/.

CHAPTER 9

Security Design in the Cloud

The only truly secure system is one that is powered off, cast in a block of concrete, and sealed in a lead-lined room with armed guards.

—GENE SPAFFORD, PROFESSOR, PURDUE UNIVERSITY

Prior to cloud computing, buyers of commercial software products did not demand the level of security from vendors that they do today. Software that was purchased and installed locally within the enterprise provided various security features for the buyer to configure in order to secure the application. The vendors would make it easy to integrate with enterprise security data stores such as Active Directory and provide single sign-on (SSO) capabilities and other features so that buyers could configure the software to meet their security requirements. These commercial software products were run within the buyer's perimeter behind the corporate firewall. With cloud computing, vendors have a greater responsibility to secure the software on behalf of the cloud consumers. Since consumers are giving up control and often allowing their data to live outside of their firewall, they are now requiring that the vendors comply with various regulations. Building enterprise software in the cloud today requires a heavy focus on security. This is a welcome change for those of us who have been waving the red flag the past several years about the lack of focus on application security in the enterprise. There is a common myth that critical data in the cloud cannot be secure. The reality is that security must be architected into the system regardless of where the data lives. It is not a matter of where the data resides; it is a matter of how much security is built into the cloud service.

This chapter will discuss the impacts of data as it pertains to cloud security and both the real and perceived ramifications. From there, we will discuss how much security is required— an amount that is different for every project. Then we will discuss the responsibilities of both the cloud service provider and the cloud service consumer for each cloud service model. Finally, we will discuss security strategies for these focus areas: policy enforcement, encryption, key management, web security, application programming interface (API) management, patch management, logging, monitoring, and auditing.

The Truth about Data in the Cloud

Many companies are quick to write off building services in the public cloud because of the belief that data outside of their firewalls cannot be secured and cannot meet the requirements of regulations such as PCI DSS (Payment Card Industry Data Security Standard) and HIPAA (Health Information Portability and Accountability Act). The fact is, none of these regulations declare where the data can and cannot reside. What the regulations do dictate is that PII (personally identifiable information) such as demographic data, credit card numbers, or health-related information must be encrypted at all times. These requirements can be met regardless of whether the data lives in the public cloud.

The next issue deals with a government's ability to seize data from cloud service providers. In the United States, the USA Patriot Act of 2001 was made law shortly after the 2001 terrorist attacks on the World Trade Center. This law gave the U.S. government unprecedented access to request data from any U.S.-based company regardless of what country its data center is in. In other words, any U.S.-based company with a global presence is required by law to comply with the U.S. government's request for data even if the data contains information for non-U.S. citizens on servers outside of U.S. soil. Many other countries have similar laws even though these laws are not as highly publicized as the Patriot Act.

Due to laws like the Patriot Act, many companies make the assumption that they just cannot put their data at risk by allowing a cloud service provider to store the data on their behalf. This assumption is only partially true and can easily be mitigated. First, the government can request data from any company regardless of whether the data is in the cloud. Keeping the data on-premises does not protect a company from being subject to a government request for data. Second, it is true that the odds of a company being impacted by a government search increase if the data is in a shared environment with many other customers. However, if a company encrypts its data, the government would have to request that the company unencrypts the data so that it can inspect it. Encrypting data is the best way to mitigate the risks of government requests for data and invalidates the myth that critical data can't live in the public cloud.

In June 2013, Edward Snowden, a contractor working for the National Security Agency (NSA) in the United States, leaked documents that revealed that the NSA was extracting large volumes of data from major U.S. companies such as Verizon, Facebook, Google, Microsoft, and others. Many people interpreted this news to mean that the public cloud was no longer safe. What many people did not realize was that much of the data that was retrieved from these big companies' data centers was not hosted in the public cloud. For example, Verizon runs its own data centers and none of the phone call metadata that the government retrieved from Verizon was from servers in the cloud. The same holds true for Facebook, which owns its own private cloud. The reality is that no data is safe anywhere from a request for data by government agencies when national security is at stake.

How Much Security Is Required

The level of security required for a cloud-based application or service depends on numerous factors such as:

- Target industry
- Customer expectations
- Sensitivity of data being stored
- Risk tolerance
- Maturity of product
- Transmission boundaries

The target industry often determines what regulations are in scope. For example, if the cloud services being built are in the health care, government, or financial industries, the level of security required is usually very high. If the cloud services are in the online games or social web industries, the level of security required is likely more moderate. Business-to-business (B2B) services typically require a higher level of security, because most companies consuming cloud services require that all third-party vendors meet a minimum set of security requirements. Consumer-facing services or business-to-consumer (B2C) services usually offer a use-at-your-own-risk service with terms of service that focus on privacy but make very limited promises about security and regulations. For example, Facebook has a terms-of-service agreement that states that the security of your account is your responsibility. Facebook gives you a list of 10 things you agree to if you accept its terms of service.

Customer expectation is an interesting factor when determining how much security and controls to put in place. Sometimes it is the customers' perception of the cloud that can drive the security requirements. For example, a company may plan on building its solution 100 percent in a public cloud but encounters an important, large client that refuses to have any of its data in the public cloud. If the client is important enough, the company may decide to adopt a hybrid cloud approach in order not to lose this customer even though there might be no reason other than customer preference driving that decision. This is common for both retail and health care customers. In the two start-ups that I worked at, both were deployed 100 percent in the public cloud until we encountered some very profitable and important customers that forced us to run some of our services in a private data center.

The sensitivity of the data within cloud services has a major impact on the security requirements. Social media data such as tweets, photos from photo-sharing applications like Instagram and Pinterest, and Facebook wall messages are all public information. Users agree that this information is public when they accept the terms of service. These social media services do not have the requirement to encrypt the data at rest in the database. Companies processing medical claims, payments, top-secret government information, and biometric data will be subject to regulatory controls that require encryption of data at rest in the database and a higher level of process and controls in the data center.

Risk tolerance can drive security requirements, as well. Some companies may feel that a security breach would be so disruptive to their businesses, create such bad public relations, and damage customer satisfaction so much that they apply the strongest security controls even though the industry and the customers don't demand it. A start-up or smaller company may be very risk tolerant and rank getting to market quickly at a low cost as a higher priority than investing heavily in security. A larger company may rank strong security controls higher than speed-to-market because of the amount of publicity it would receive if it had a breach and the impact of that publicity on its shareholders and customers.

The maturity of the product often drives security requirements, as well. Building products is an evolutionary process. Often, companies have a product roadmap that balances business features with technical requirements like security, scalability, and so on. Many products don't need the highest level of security and scalability on day one but will eventually need to add these features over time as the product matures and gains more traction in the marketplace.

Transmission boundaries refer to what endpoints the data travels to and from. A cloud service that is used internally within a company where both endpoints are contained within the company's virtual private network (VPN) will require much less security than a cloud service that travels outside of the company's data center over the Internet. Data that crosses international boundaries can be required to address country-specific security requirements. The U.S.-EU Safe Harbor regulation requires U.S. companies to comply with the EU Data Protection Directive controls in order to transfer personal data outside the European Union. As of the writing of this book, U.S. companies self-certify. After the recent NSA scandal, this law could change in the near future and a formal certification may be required.

Once a company considers these factors and determines how much security is required for its cloud service, the next questions to ask are who is going to do the work (build versus buy), how will the security requirements be met, and by when is it needed. For each security requirement there should be an evaluation to determine if there is a solution available in the marketplace or if the requirement should be met by building the solution internally. There are many open source, commercial, and Software as a Service (SaaS)–based security solutions in the marketplace today. Security is a dynamic field and keeping software current enough to address the most recent security threats and best practices is a daunting task. A best practice is to leverage a combination of open source or commercial products or Security as a Service (SecaaS)–based software to meet requirements such as SSO, federated security, intrusion detection, intrusion prevention, encryption, and more.

AEA CASE STUDY: Determining the Level of Security Required

Acme eAuction's (AEA) target industry is e-commerce auction and retail. This industry has embraced doing business over the Internet for years and was also an early adopter of cloud computing. Auction sites like eBay and e-commerce sites like Amazon have been selling goods and services in the cloud for years.

Buyers and sellers will be not be opposed to using AEA's services if they are deployed in the cloud. They will, however, expect their personal information, credit card information, and financial transactions to be protected against misuse and theft. Channel partners, affiliate networks, and App Store developers will expect secure access to the platform's APIs and expect that all data transmitted between the two parties will be over a secure protocol.

To avoid having the entire auction platform falling under scope of PCI DSS regulations, AEA chose to off-load all credit card business processes to a certified third-party SecaaS solution. The AEA auction platform integrates with this trusted SecaaS solution, which manages the consumers' credit card transactions and returns a hash-key value to AEA. AEA stores this hashed value in its database and never sees the actual credit card anywhere on the platform.

After analyzing the requirements of all of the external partners and customers, AEA realizes that building and maintaining authorization and authentication services for external accounts is a challenging task. Each external party may support a different technology stack and use various protocols for communicating. Instead of building all of the code to support these permutations, AEA chose to select a SecaaS solution to manage the security of all of these endpoints. Another factor for this decision was that AEA has a low tolerance for risk, knowing that a major security breach could create a huge loss of business and expose it to a lot of bad publicity.

Responsibilities for Each Cloud Service Model

When leveraging the cloud, the cloud service consumer (CSC) and the cloud service provider (CSP) have a shared responsibility for securing the cloud services. As shown in Figure 9.1, the further up the cloud stack consumers go, the more they shift the responsibility to the provider.

The cloud stack consists of four categories. At the bottom is the infrastructure layer, which is made up of physical things like data centers, server-related hardware and peripherals, network infrastructure, storage devices, and more. Companies that are not leveraging cloud computing or are building their own private clouds have to provide the security for all of this physical

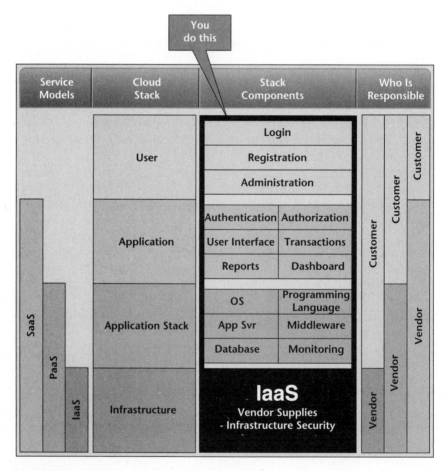

Figure 9.1 Infrastructure as a Service

infrastructure. For those companies leveraging a public cloud solution, the public cloud service provider manages the physical infrastructure security on behalf of the consumer.

Some companies might cringe at the thought of outsourcing infrastructure security to a vendor, but the fact of the matter is most public Infrastructure as a Service (IaaS) providers invest a substantial amount of time, money, and human capital into providing world-class security at levels far greater than most cloud consumers can feasibly provide. For example, Amazon Web Services (AWS) has been certified in ISO 27001, HIPAA, PCI, FISO, SSAE 16, FedRAMP, ITAR, FIPS, and other regulations. Many companies would be hard pressed to invest in that amount of security and auditing within their data centers.

As we move up to the application stack layer, where PaaS solutions take root, we see a shift in responsibility to the providers for securing the underlying application software, such as operating systems, application servers, database software, and programming languages like .NET, Ruby, Python, Java, and many others. There are a number of other application stack tools that provide on-demand services like caching, queuing, messaging, e-mail, logging, monitoring, and others. In an IaaS service model, the service consumer would own managing and securing all of these services, but with Platform as a Service (PaaS), this is all handled by the service provider in some cases. Let's elaborate.

There are actually six distinct deployment models for PaaS, as shown in Figure 9.2.

The public hosted deployment model is where the provider provides the IaaS in the provider's own public cloud. Examples are Google App Engine, Force.com, and Microsoft Azure. In this model, the provider is responsible for all of the security for both the infrastructure and application stack. In some cases, the PaaS provider runs on top of another provider's infrastructure. For example, Heroku and Engine Yard both run on AWS. In the consumers' eyes, the PaaS provider is responsible for all of the infrastructure and application stack security, but in reality, the PaaS provider manages the application stack security but leverages the IaaS provider to provide the infrastructure security. In the public-hosted model, only the PaaS provider is responsible for securing the actual PaaS software. The PaaS software is a shared service consumed by all PaaS consumers.

The public-managed deployment model is where the PaaS provider deploys on a public cloud of the CSC's choice and hires the PaaS provider or some other third party to manage the PaaS software and the application stack on its behalf. (Note: Not all PaaS providers have the ability to run on multiple public clouds.) In the public-managed model, the PaaS software needs to be managed by the customer, meaning it is up to the customer and its managed service provider to determine when to update the PaaS software when patches and fixes come out. Although the consumer still shifts the responsibility of

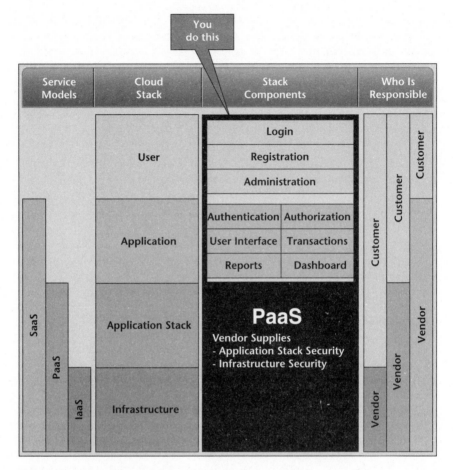

Figure 9.2 Platform as a Service

security for the PaaS software and the application stack, the consumer is still involved in the process of updating software. In the public-hosted model, this all happens transparently to the consumer.

The public-unmanaged deployment model is where the PaaS provider deploys on an IaaS provider's public cloud, and the consumer takes the responsibility of managing and patching both the PaaS software and application stack. This is a common deployment model within enterprises when a hybrid cloud is chosen. Often with a hybrid PaaS solution, the consumer must choose a PaaS that can be deployed in any cloud, public or private. PaaS providers that meet this requirement only deliver PaaS as software and do not handle the infrastructure layer. An example of this model would be deploying an open-source PaaS like Red Hat's OpenShift on top of an open source IaaS solution like OpenStack, which can be deployed both within the consumer's data center for some workloads and in a public cloud IaaS provider like Rackspace for other workloads.

The private-hosted model is where a private PaaS is deployed on an externally hosted private IaaS cloud. In this model the consumer shifts the responsibility of the infrastructure layer to the IaaS provider, but still owns managing and securing the application stack and the PaaS software. An example of this model would be deploying an open source PaaS like Cloud Foundry on top of an open source IaaS solution like OpenStack, which can be deployed in a private cloud IaaS provider like Rackspace for other workloads. (Note: Rackspace provides both public and private IaaS solutions.)

The private-managed model is similar to the public-hosted model except that the IaaS cloud is a private cloud, either externally hosted or within the consumer's own data center. If the IaaS cloud is externally hosted, then the only difference between the private-hosted and the private-managed model is that the consumer hires a service provider to manage and secure the PaaS and application stack and relies on the IaaS provider to manage and secure the infrastructure layer. If the IaaS cloud is internal, then the consumer owns the responsibility for managing and securing the infrastructure layer, while the managed service provider manages and secures the PaaS software and the application stack.

The private-unmanaged model is where the consumer is in charge of securing the entire cloud stack plus the PaaS software. In reality, this is a private IaaS with the addition of managing a PaaS solution in the data center. This is a popular option for enterprises that want to keep data out of the public cloud and want to own the security responsibility. Another reason is the consumer may want to run on specific hardware specifications not available in the public cloud or it may want to shift certain workloads to bare-metal (non-virtualized) machines to gain performance improvements. An example of this model is deploying a .NET PaaS like Apprenda on top of OpenStack running in an internal private cloud.

The next layer up is the application layer. This is where application development must focus on things like using secure transmission protocols (https, sFTP, etc.), encrypting data, authenticating and authorizing users, protecting against web vulnerabilities, and much more. For SaaS solutions, the responsibility for application security shifts to the provider as shown in Figure 9.3.

At the top of the stack is the user layer. At this layer the consumer performs user administration tasks such as adding users to a SaaS application, assigning roles to a user, granting access to allow developers to build on top of cloud services, and so on. In some cases, the end user may be responsible for managing its own users. For example, a consumer may build a SaaS solution on top of a PaaS or IaaS provider and allow its customers to self-manage access within their own organizations.

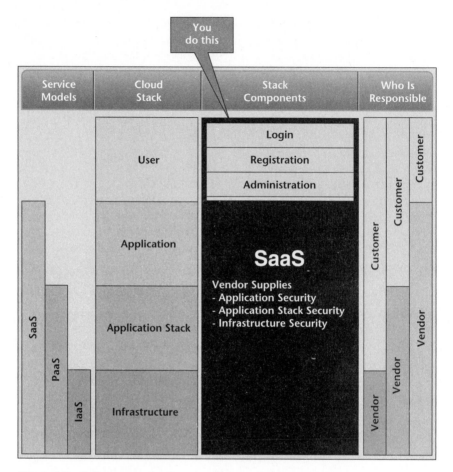

Figure 9.3   Software as a Service

To sum up the security responsibilities, choosing cloud service and cloud deployment models determines which responsibilities are owned by the provider and which are owned by the consumer. Once a consumer determines what the provider is responsible for, it should then evaluate the provider's security controls and accreditations to determine whether the provider can meet the desired security requirements.

Security Strategies

Most applications built in the cloud, public or private, are distributed in nature. The reason many applications are built like this is so they can be programmed to scale horizontally as demand goes up. A typical cloud architecture may have a dedicated web server farm, a web service farm, a caching server farm, and a database server farm. In addition, each farm may be redundant across multiple data centers, physical or virtual. As one can imagine, the number of servers in a scalable cloud architecture can grow to a high level. This is why a company should apply the following three key strategies for managing security in a cloud-based application:

1. Centralization
2. Standardization
3. Automation

Centralization refers to the practice of consolidating a set of security controls, processes, policies, and services and reducing the number of places where security needs to be managed and implemented. For example, a common set of services should be built for allowing users to be authenticated and authorized to use cloud services as opposed to having each application provide different solutions. All of the security controls related to the application stack should be administered from one place, as well.

Here is an analogy to explain centralization. A grocery store has doors in two parts of the building. There are front doors, which are the only doors that customers (users) can come in and there are back doors where shipments (deployments) and maintenance workers (systems administrators) enter. The rest of the building is double solid concrete walls with security cameras everywhere. The back door is heavily secured and only authorized personnel with the appropriate badge can enter. The front door has some basic protections like double pane glass, but any customer willing to spend money is welcome during hours of operation. If the grocery store changes its hours of operation (policy), it simply changes a time setting in the alarm system as to when the doors lock. This same mentality should be applied to cloud-based systems. There should be a limited way for people or systems to get access. Customers should all enter the same way through one place where they can be monitored. IT people who need access should have a single point of entry with the appropriate controls and credentials required to enter parts of the system that no others can. Finally, policies should be centralized and configurable so changes can be made and tracked consistently and quickly.

Standardization is the next important strategy. Security should be thought of as a core service that can be shared across the enterprise, not a solution for a specific application. Each application having its own unique security solutions is the equivalent of adding doors all over the side of the building in the grocery store analogy. Companies should look at implementing industry standards for accessing systems, such as OAuth and OpenID, when connecting to third parties. Leveraging standard application protocols like Lightweight Directory Access Protocol (LDAP) for querying and modifying directory services like Active Directory or ApacheDS is highly recommended, as well. In Chapter 10, "Creating a Centralized Logging Strategy," we will discuss standards around log and error messages.

Standardization applies to three areas. First, we should subscribe to industry best practices when it comes to implementing security solutions and selecting things like the method of encryption, authorization, API tokenization, and the like. Second, security should be implemented as a stand-alone set of services that are shared across applications. Third, all of the security data outputs (logs, errors, warnings, debugging data, etc.) should follow standard naming conventions and formats (we will discuss this more in Chapter 10).

The third strategy is automation. A great example of the need for automation comes from the book called *The Phoenix Project*. This book tells a fictional, yet relevant, story of a company whose IT department was always missing dates and never finding time to implement technical requirements such as a large number of security tasks. Over time, they started figuring out what steps were repeatable so that they could automate them. Once they automated the process for creating environments and deploying software, they were able to implement the proper security controls and process within the automation steps. Before they implemented automation, development and deployments took so much time that they never had enough time left in their sprints to focus on nonfunctional requirements such as security.

Another reason automation is so important is because in order to automatically scale as demand increases or decreases, virtual machines and code deployments must be scripted so that no human intervention is required to keep up with demand. All cloud infrastructure resources should be created from automated scripts to ensure that the latest security patches and controls are automatically in place as resources are created on-demand. If provisioning new resources requires manual intervention, the risks of exposing gaps in security increase due to human error.

Areas of Focus

In addition to the three security strategies, a strategy I call PDP, which consists of three distinct actions, must be implemented. Those three actions are:

1. Protection
2. Detection
3. Prevention

Protection is the first area of focus and is one that most people are familiar with. This is where we implement all of the security controls, policies, and processes to protect the system and the company from security breaches. Detection is the process of mining logs, triggering events, and proactively trying to find security vulnerabilities within the systems. The third action is prevention, where if we detect something, we must take the necessary steps to prevent further damage. For example, if we see a pattern where a large number of failed attempts are being generated by a particular IP, we must implement the necessary steps to block that IP to prevent any damage. As an auditor once told me, "It's nice that your intrusion detection tools detected that these IPs are trying to log into your systems, but what are you going to do about it? Where is the intrusion prevention?"

In order to secure cloud-based systems, there are a number of areas to focus the security controls on. Here are some of the most important areas:

- Policy enforcement
- Encryption
- Key management
- Web security
- API management
- Patch management
- Logging
- Monitoring
- Auditing

Policy Enforcement

Policies are rules that are used to manage security within a system. A best practice is to make these rules configurable and decouple them from the applications that use them. Policies are maintained at every layer of the cloud stack. At the user layer, access policies are often maintained in a central data store like Active Directory, where user information is maintained and accessed through protocols like LDAP. Changes to user data and rules should be managed within the central data store and not within the application, unless the rules are specific to the application.

At the application layer, application-specific rules should also be maintained in a centralized data store abstracted from the actual application. The application should access its own central data store, which can be managed by a database, an XML file, a registry, or some other method, via API so that if the policies change, they can be changed in one place.

At the application stack layer, operating systems, databases, application servers, and development languages all are configurable already. The key to policy enforcement at this level is automation. In an IaaS environment, this is accomplished by scripting the infrastructure provisioning process. A best practice is to create a template for each unique machine image that contains all of the security policies around access, port management, encryption, and so on. This template, often referred to as the "gold image," is used to build the cloud servers that run the application stack and the applications. When policies change, the gold image is updated to reflect those changes. Then new servers are provisioned while the old, outdated servers are deprovisioned. This entire process can be scripted to be fully automated to eliminate human error. This method is much easier than trying to upgrade or patch existing servers, especially in an environment that has hundreds or thousands of servers.

Recommendation: Identify policies at each layer of the cloud stack. Isolate policies into a centralized data store. Standardize all access to policies (e.g., API, standard protocols, or scripts). Automate policies when the steps are repeatable (e.g., golden image, deployments).

Encryption

Sensitive data processed in the cloud should always be encrypted. Any message that is processed over the Internet that contains sensitive data should use a secure protocol such as https, sFTP, or SSL. But securing data in transit is not enough. Some attributes will need to be encrypted at rest. *At rest* refers to where the data is stored. Often data is stored in a database, but sometimes it is stored as a file on a file system.

Encryption protects data from being read by the naked eye, but it comes at a cost. For an application to understand the contents of the data, the data must be unencrypted to be read, which adds time to the process. Because of this, simply encrypting every attribute is often not feasible. What is required is that personally identifiable information (PII) data is encrypted. Here are the types of data that fall under PII:

- Demographics information (full name, Social Security number, address, etc.)
- Health information (biometrics, medications, medical history, etc.)
- Financial information (credit card numbers, bank account numbers, etc.)

It is also wise to encrypt any attributes that might give hints to an unauthorized user about system information that could aid in attacks. Examples of this kind of information are:

- IP addresses
- Server names
- Passwords
- Keys

There are a variety of ways to handle encryption. In a database, sensitive data can be encrypted at the attribute level, the row level, or the table level. At one start-up that I worked at, we were maintaining biometric data for employees of our corporate customers who had opted into our health and wellness application. The biometric data was only needed the first time the employee logged onto the system. What we decided to do was create an employee-biometric table that related back to the employee table that isolated all of the PII data to a single table and encrypted that table only. This gave us the following advantages:

- **Simplicity**. We could manage encryption at the table level.
- **Performance**. We kept encryption out of the employee table, which was accessed frequently and for many different reasons.
- **Traceability**. It is much easier to produce proof of privacy since all attributes in scope are isolated and all API calls to the table are tracked.

For sensitive data that is stored outside of databases, there are many options, as well. The data can be encrypted before transmission and stored in its encrypted state. The file system or folder structure that the data is stored in can be encrypted. When files are accessed they can be password protected and require a key to unencrypt. Also, there are many cloud storage providers that provide certified storage services where data can be sent securely to the cloud service where it is encrypted and protected. These types of services are often used to store medical records for HIPAA compliance.

Recommendation: Identify all sensitive data that flows in and out of the system. Encrypt all sensitive data in flight and at rest. Design for simplicity and performance. Isolate sensitive data where it makes sense to minimize the amount of access and to minimize performance issues due to frequent decryption. Evaluate cloud vendors to ensure that they can provide the level of encryption your application requires.

Key Management

Key management is a broad topic that could merit its own chapter, but I will cover it at a high level. For this discussion, I will focus on public and private *key pairs*. The public and private keys are two uniquely and mathematically related cryptographic keys. Whatever object is protected by a public key can only be decrypted by the corresponding private key and vice versa. The advantage of using public–private key pairs is that if an authorized person or system gets access to the data, they cannot decrypt and use the data without the corresponding keys. This is why I recommend using encryption and keys to protect against the Patriot Act and other government surveillance policies that many countries have.

A critical part of maintaining secure systems is the management of these keys. There are some basic rules to follow to ensure that the keys do not get discovered by people or systems without permission. After all, keys are worthless if they are in the hands of the wrong people. Here are some best practices.

Keys should not be stored in clear text. Make sure that the keys are encrypted before they are stored. Also, keys should not be referenced directly in the code. Centralized policy management should be applied to keys, as well. Store all keys outside of the applications and provide a single secure method of requesting the keys from within the applications. When possible, keys should be rotated every 90 days. This is especially important for the keys provided by the cloud service provider. For example, when signing up for an AWS account a key pair is issued. Eventually the entire production system is deployed under this single account. Imagine the damage if the key for the AWS account got into the wrong hands. If keys are never rotated, there is a risk when people leave the company and still know the keys. Key rotation should be an automated process so it can be executed during critical situations. For example, let's say that one of the systems within the cloud environment was compromised. Once the threat was removed it would be wise to rotate the keys right away to mitigate the risk in case the keys were stolen. Also, if an employee who had access to the keys leaves the company, the keys should be rotated immediately.

Another best practice is to make sure that the keys are never stored on the same servers that they are protecting. For example, if a public–private key pair is being used to protect access to a database, don't store the keys on the database server. Keys should be stored in an isolated, protected environment that has limited access, has a backup and recovery plan, and is fully auditable. A loss of a key is equivalent to losing the data because without the keys, nobody can decipher the contents of the data.

Recommendation: Identify all the areas within the system that require public–private key pairs. Implement a key management strategy that includes the best practices of policy management discussed earlier. Make sure keys are not stored in clear text, are rotated regularly, and are centrally managed in a highly secure data store with limited access.

Web Security

One of the most common ways that systems get compromised is through web-based systems. Without the proper level of security, unauthorized people and systems can intercept data in transit, inject SQL statements, hijack user sessions, and perform all kinds of malicious behaviors. Web security is a very dynamic area because as soon as the industry figures out how to address a current threat, the attackers figure out a new way to attack. A best practice for companies building web applications is to leverage the web frameworks for the corresponding application stack. For example, Microsoft developers should leverage the .NET framework, PHP developers should leverage a framework like Zend, Python developers would be wise to leverage the Django framework, and Ruby developers can leverage Rails.

The frameworks are not the answer to web security; there is much more security design that goes into building secure systems (and I touch on many of them in this chapter). However, most of these frameworks do a very good job of protecting against the top 10 web threats. The key is to ensure that you are using the most recent version of the framework and keep up with the patches because security is a moving target.

It is also wise to leverage a web vulnerability scanning service. There are SaaS solutions for performing these types of scans. They run continuously and report on vulnerabilities. They rank the severity of the vulnerabilities and provide detailed information of both the issue and some recommended solutions. In some cases, cloud service consumers may demand web vulnerability scanning in their contracts. In one of my start-ups, it was common for customers to demand scans because of the sensitivity of the types of data we were processing.

Recommendation: Leverage updated web frameworks to protect against the top 10 web vulnerabilities. Proactively and continuously run vulnerability scans to detect security gaps and address them before they are discovered by those with malicious intent. Understand that these frameworks will not guarantee that the systems are secure but will improve the security of the web applications immensely over rolling your own web security.

API Management

Back in Chapter 6 we discussed Representational State Transfer or RESTful web APIs in great detail. One of the advantages of cloud-based architectures is how easily different cloud services can be integrated by leveraging APIs. However, this creates some interesting security challenges because each API within the system has the potential to be accessed over the web. Luckily, a number of standards have emerged so that each company does not have to build its own API security from scratch. In fact, for companies sharing APIs with partners and customers, it is an expectation that your APIs support OAuth and OpenID. If there are scenarios where OAuth or OpenID cannot be used, use basic authentication over SSL. There are also several API management SaaS solutions that are available, such as Apigee, Mashery, and Layer7. These SaaS providers can help secure APIs as well as provide many other features such as monitoring, analytics, and more.

Here are some best practices for building APIs. Try not to use passwords and instead use API keys between the client and the provider. This approach removes the dependency on needing to maintain user passwords since they are very dynamic. The number one reason for using keys instead of passwords is that the keys are much more secure. Most passwords are no more than eight characters in length because it is hard for users to remember passwords longer than that. In addition, many users do not create strong passwords. Using keys results in a longer and more complex key value, usually 256 characters, and passwords are created by systems instead of users. The number of combinations that a password bot would need to try to figure out the password for a key value is many times greater than an eight-digit password. If you have to store passwords for some reason, make sure they are encrypted with an up-to-date encryption utility like bcrypt.

A best practice is to avoid sessions and session state to prevent session hijacking. If you are building RESTful services the correct way, this should not be hard to implement. If you are using SOAP instead of REST, then you will be required to maintain sessions and state and expose yourself to session hijacking. Another best practice is to reset authentication on every request so if an unauthorized user somehow gets authenticated, he is no longer able to access the system after that request is terminated, whereas if the authentication is not terminated, the unauthorized user can stay connected and do even more damage. The next recommendation is to base the authentication on the resource content of the request, not the URL. URLs are easier to discover and more fragile than the resource content. A common mistake that auditors pick up on is that developers often leave too much information in the resource content. Make sure that debug information is not on in production and also ensure that information describing version numbers or descriptions of the underlying application stack are excluded from the resource content. For example, an auditor once flagged one of our APIs because it disclosed the version of Apache we were running. Any information that is not needed by the service consumer should be removed from the resource content.

Recommendation: Do not roll your own security. Use industry standards like OAuth. Refrain from using passwords, always use SSL, encrypt sensitive attributes within the resource content, and only include information in the resource content that is absolutely necessary. Also evaluate Security as a Service solutions and API management solutions, and leverage them where it makes sense within the architecture.

Patch Management

Patching servers applies to the IaaS cloud service model and the private cloud deployment model. When leveraging IaaS, the cloud service consumer is responsible for the application stack and therefore must manage the security of the operating system, database server, application server, the development language, and all other software and servers that make up the system. The same is true for private PaaS solutions. For regulations that focus on security, like the SSAE16 SOC 2 audit, patching servers must be performed at least every 30 days. Not only do the servers require patching, but the auditors need to see proof that the patching occurred and a log of what patches were applied.

There are many ways to manage patching but whatever method is chosen should rely on automation as much as possible. Any time manual intervention is allowed there is a risk of not only creating issues in production but also missing or forgetting to apply certain patches. A common approach to patching is to use the golden image method described earlier. Each unique server configuration should have an image that has the most current security patches applied to it. This image should be checked into a source code repository and versioned to produce an audit trial of the changes and also allow for rollbacks in case the deployment causes issues. Every 30 days, the latest golden image should be deployed to production and the old server image should be retired. It is not recommended to apply security patches to existing servers. Live by the rule of *create new servers and destroy the old*. There are two main reasons for this strategy. First, it is much simpler and less risky to leave the existing servers untouched. Second, if major issues occur when the new images are deployed, it is much easier and safer to redeploy the previous image than to back software and patches out of the existing image.

For companies that have continuous delivery in place, patching is a much simpler undertaking. With continuous delivery, both the software and the environment are deployed together, which ensures that deployments always deploy the most recent version of the golden image. In most continuous delivery shops, software is deployed anywhere from every two weeks, to every day, and in some cases, multiple times a day. In these environments, the servers are being refreshed frequently, much less than every 30 days. A patching strategy in this scenario entails updating the golden image at least once every 30 days, but there is no need to schedule a security patch deployment because the latest golden image gets deployed regularly.

Recommendation: Create and validate a golden image that contains all of the latest and greatest security patches and check it into the source code repository at least once every 30 days. Automate the deployment process to pull the latest golden image from the source code repository and deploy both the new software and the new environment based on the golden image, while retiring the current production servers containing the previous version of the golden image. Do not try to update servers—simply replace them.

Logging, Monitoring, and Auditing

Logging refers to the collection of all system logs. Logs come from the infrastructure, the application stack, and the application. It is a best practice to write a log entry for every event that happens within a system, especially events that involve users or systems requesting access. Logging is covered in detail in Chapter 10.

Monitoring refers to the process of watching over a system through a set of tools that provide information about the health and activity occurring on a system. A best practice is to implement a set of monitors that observe activity on the system and look for security risks. Monitoring involves both looking at real-time activity and mining log files. Monitoring is covered in Chapter 12. Auditing is the process of reviewing the security processes and controls to ensure that the system is complying with the required regulatory controls and meeting the security requirements and SLAs of the system. Auditing is covered in Chapter 7.

Summary

The popularity of cloud computing has raised awareness about the importance of building secure applications and services. The level of responsibility a cloud service provider takes on depends on which cloud service model and deployment model is chosen by the cloud service consumer. Consumers must not rely solely on their providers for security. Instead, consumers must take a three-pronged approach to security by applying security best practices to the applications and services, monitoring and detecting security issues, and practicing security prevention by actively addressing issues found by monitoring logs. Providers provide the tools to build highly secure applications and services. Consumers building solutions on top of providers must use these tools to build in the proper level of security and comply with the regulations demanded by their customers.

References

Barker, E., W. Barker, W. Burr, W. Polk, and M. Smid (2007, March). "Computer Security: NIST Special Publication 800–57." Retrieved from http://csrc.nist.gov/publications/nistpubs/800–57/sp800–57-Part1-revised2_Mar08–2007.pdf.

Chickowski, E. (2013, February 12). "Database Encryption Depends on Effective Key Management." Retrieved from http://www.darkreading.com/database/database-encryption-depends-on-effective/240148441.

Hazelwood, Les (2012, July). "Designing a Beautiful REST+JSON API." San Francisco. Retrieved from https://www.youtube.com/watch?v=5WXYw4J4QOU&list=PL22B1B879CCC56461&index=9.

Kim, G., K. Behr, and G. Spafford (2013). *The Phoenix Project: A Novel About IT, DevOps and Helping Your Business Win*. Portland, OR: IT Revolution Press.

CHAPTER 10

Creating a Centralized Logging Strategy

The problem with troubleshooting is trouble shoots back.

—Anonymous

Logging is a critical component of any cloud-based application. As we shift away from the old client-server architectures to cloud-based distributed architectures, managing systems becomes more complex. Many cloud-based systems are built to scale up and down on-demand. Under the covers, compute resources are automatically being provisioned and deprovisioned as workloads spike up and down. The dynamic nature of an elastic cloud application creates a need to separate the storing of logging information from the physical servers where the logs are created so that the information is not lost when the cloud resources go away.

This chapter will discuss the uses of log files and the requirements for building a centralized logging strategy.

Log File Uses

For those of us building highly distributed systems in the cloud, having a sound logging strategy is a critical component of building a secure and manageable solution. Log files have very useful information about the behavior of database activity, user access, error and debugging information, and much more. In a distributed environment where a company may have tens, hundreds, or even thousands of servers that make up its overall solution, finding data in logs is like finding a needle in a haystack without a centralized logging solution.

Log files have many uses. Here is a core list of uses of log files in most systems:

- **Troubleshooting**. Debugging information and error messages are collected for analyzing what is occurring in the production environment.

- **Security**. Tracking all user access, both successful and unsuccessful access attempts. Intrusion detection and fraud detection analysis depends on collecting logs.
- **Auditing**. Providing a trail of data for auditors is mandatory for passing audits. Having documentation of processes and controls is not enough to pass an audit. Those documents need to be backed up with real data from the logs.
- **Monitoring**. Identifying trends, anomalies, thresholds, and other variables proactively allows companies to resolve issues before they become noticeable and before they impact end users.

The adoption of the cloud has led to the much-needed awareness of application and system security, which unfortunately had not been a high enough priority in many enterprises in the past. Many companies felt secure behind their firewalls but in reality they often had huge security vulnerabilities due to the lack of application security. Now with security in the forefront, companies building solutions in the cloud are rightfully being held to the highest standards, such as ISO 27001, SSAE-16, PCI, and others. Anybody who has ever been through one of these audits knows that locking down access to production servers is a must. In order to do that a company must have a logging strategy that centrally maintains the logs on a separate server farm so that the administrators can remove developer access from all production servers. Without a logging strategy, a company will have to allow developers and operations personnel to access production servers, which will get flagged in an audit. This is an extremely risky situation both from a security standpoint and because of the possibility of human error.

Logging Requirements

There are two key requirements for architecting a centralized logging strategy.

Direct Logs to an Isolated Storage Area

The first requirement is to direct all logs to a redundant and isolated storage area. In an Infrastructure as a Service (IaaS) implementation, a design for a centralized logging solution might look like that depicted in Figure 10.1.

In this design, all logs are directed to syslog instead of being written directly to disk on the local machine. Syslog on each server is piped directly to a dedicated logging server farm. The logging server farm should be redundant across data centers, or availability zones (AZ) as they are called on Amazon Web Services. Once the data arrives on the logging server farm there are a

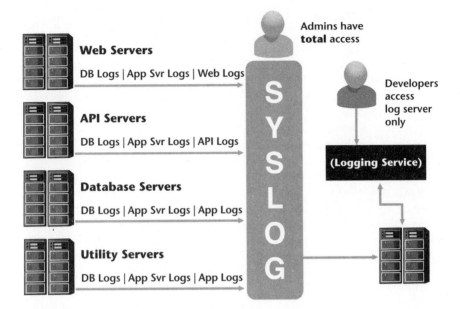

Figure 10.1   Centralized Logging Strategy

number of logging solutions, both open source and commercial, that transform the data into a NoSQL database. These tools also provide a rich user interface that allows the end user to search the logs and schedule jobs, trigger alerts, create reports, and much more. This strategy provides the following benefits:

- Allows the administrators to block all developer access from all servers in the production environment. Developers can only access production logging servers and only through a secure user interface (UI) or through application programming interface (API) access.
- Auditing becomes much simpler since all logs are in one place.
- Data mining and trend analysis become feasible because all logging data is stored in a NoSQL database.
- Implementing intrusion detection becomes simpler because tools can be run on top of the central logging database.
- Loss of log data is minimized because data is not stored on local disk of servers that may be deprovisioned on the fly.

For applications built on top of IaaS, there are a few options. If the application team wants to build and manage its own logging solution, it will need to stand up a logging server (or two or more for redundancy) and configure the operating system to use a command like syslogd for Linux-based systems, log4J for Apache, or Log4Net for .NET. These are just a few of many tools for assisting with logging. Once the logs are all routed to a central repository, there are many open source and commercial products that can be used that sit on top of the central repository and provide easy-to-use searching, job scheduling, event processing, and notification capabilities for sifting through log data.

Another option is to leverage a Software as a Service (SaaS) logging solution. In this model the logs are sent to a cloud-based centralized logging Database as a Service solution. SaaS logging solutions have many advantages. First, the team no longer has to build, manage, and maintain logging functionality, which is usually not a core competency. Second, the logs are maintained off-site on a scalable, reliable third party's cloud infrastructure. Third, if any part of the data center goes down, the logs service will not be impacted. If a company is leveraging more than one cloud platform (for example, AWS and Rackspace), SaaS logging solutions are even more attractive because the log files from the different cloud service providers' (CSPs') cloud platforms can be managed and maintained in one place.

Many Platform as a Service (PaaS) solutions are integrated with the most popular logging SaaS solutions, like Loggly and Logentries, which provide API access to the central logging solution. Instead of building and managing logging services, a PaaS user can simply pay for what it uses. Logging add-ons, or plug-ins, as these are often called on PaaS platforms, are one of the reasons why PaaS is so attractive to developers. Developers can simply turn on plug-ins like logging, monitoring, Database as a Service, message queues, payment services, and more without having to write all of that code or figure out how to integrate with these solutions.

Some companies may choose to manage the logs themselves because they do not want any of their data to leave their premises. These companies are trading control for speed-to-market since they are taking on much more work than they would have to do had they gone with the SaaS solution. Another advantage of leveraging a SaaS solution for logging becomes clear when the CSP has an outage. If a company is managing the logging system on that CSP's infrastructure, the logging solution might be down, as well. Without access to the logs it will likely be incredibly difficult to troubleshoot the issues that the outage is causing. In the SaaS model, all the logs would be available during the CSP outage.

Standardize Log Formats

The second key requirement of a centralized logging strategy is to standardize all log formats, naming conventions, severity levels, and error codes for all messages. Storing all logs in a central location is a good start, but if

Table 10.1   RFC 5424 Severity Codes

Code	Severity
0	Emergency, system is unusable
1	Alert: action must be taken immediately
2	Critical: critical conditions
3	Error: error conditions
4	Warning: warning conditions
5	Notice: normal but significant condition
6	Informational: informational messages
7	Debug: debug-level messages

Source: tools.ieft.org/html/rfc5424.

the actual log messages are not designed in a standard way, the value of the data is very limited. A best practice is to build a utility service for writing application messages with a common log message format. In addition, APIs should be designed to use standard http error codes and leverage a standard like the RFC 5424 Syslog protocol to standardize on severity levels. See Table 10.1.

Finally, create a common vocabulary for error descriptions including tracking attributes such as date, time, server, module, or API name and consistently use the same terms. For example, if a system has numerous areas where IDs are being authenticated, always use the same terms, such as *authentication failed* or *access denied*. If the same terms are always used, then a simple search from the logging tools will provide consistent results. One way to enforce consistent naming is to use a database or XML data store that the developers can pull from. This eliminates the chance that developers use different descriptions, which would diminish the value of the logging data. Also, by storing these attributes in a data store, changes can be made to the data without the need for a build or a deployment.

Standards are crucial for optimizing searches and producing consistent results. The more that the data contained in log messages is standardized, the more automation can be designed. Instead of being reactive and paying people to search for anomalies in the logs, jobs can be run to detect patterns and alert the appropriate personnel if the log content is inconsistent. Audit reports can be automatically generated. Trend reports can be derived, detecting common issues. Statistics can be tied to deployments to proactively analyze the quality of each deployment. There is no end to the number of proactive insights that can be programmed if all log data is standardized. This is a key strategy for increasing automation and proactive monitoring, which leads to higher service level agreements (SLAs) and customer satisfaction.

AEA CASE STUDY: Logging Strategy Considerations

In assessing its logging strategy, Acme eAuctions (AEA) took the following items into consideration:

- Lock all developers out of the production servers for security and risk reasons.
- Need the ability to break out logs by actor (channel partner, App Store developer, affiliate network, AEA).
- AEA users can see the logs of all actors, but external actors can only see their own logs.
- Standard logging and error messages must be created and published to external actors.
- Monitoring services will be mining log data looking for patterns to raise alerts and warnings.
- External partners building on top of APIs will need log access for troubleshooting.

Based on these requirements and the fact that logging is not a core competency of AEA, AEA has chosen to evaluate cloud-based logging solutions. The logging solutions will need to support API access so the monitoring solutions can access the data in the log files. By leveraging a centralized logging solution, all production servers can be locked down so that no developers, internal or external, will have any access to the servers. External partners will be given restricted access so that they can only see their own data. AEA will be able to configure the logging solution and put it in place much quicker than if it had to build it itself. This leaves AEA more time to focus on its core, which is to build a great user experience for auction enthusiasts and provide a highly scalable and reliable website.

Summary

Log files are a critical part of any cloud-based system. Making logs easily accessible, consistent, meaningful, searchable, and centrally managed is a core strategy of any cloud implementation. Logging is often an afterthought in many systems. It should be thought of as a critical component required for security and SLA management and should be designed in from the start.

Logging is a vital piece of plumbing for IaaS, PaaS, and SaaS cloud service models. As with the construction of any house or building, plumbing is a fundamental piece of the blueprint. No builder would add pipes after hanging the drywall. No cloud application should wait until the end to implement logging.

Reference

Gerhards, R. (2009). "The Syslog Protocol." Retrieved from http://tools.ietf.org/html/rfc5424.

CHAPTER 11

SLA Management

If you think good architecture is expensive, try bad architecture.
—BRIAN FOOTE AND JOSEPH YODER

A service level agreement (SLA) is an agreement between the cloud service provider (CSP) and the cloud service consumer (CSC) that sets the expectation of the level of service that the CSP promises to provide to the CSC. SLAs are critical for cloud-based services because the CSPs take on responsibilities on behalf of the consumer. Consumers need assurance that the CSP will provide services that are reliable, secure, scalable, and available. There are two sides to this coin when it comes to SLAs. On one side, a company building cloud services on top of an Infrastructure as a Service (IaaS) or Platform as a Service (PaaS) provider has to consider the SLAs of its CSPs. The other side of the coin is the company needs to establish SLAs that can satisfy the needs of its customer base. This chapter reviews steps for defining SLAs.

Factors That Impact SLAs

SLAs in the cloud can be rather complex, especially when multiple CSPs are involved in the makeup of a cloud service. It is not uncommon that a company builds a solution that is made up of cloud services of each cloud service model. For example, our fictitious start-up, Acme eAuctions (AEA), uses an IaaS CSP to provide the infrastructure layer, a PaaS provider to provide the application stack layer, and a collection of Software as a Service (SaaS) solutions and third-party APIs for various core utility functions. Each one of these CSPs that make up the overall AEA platform has its own SLAs. AEA must take all of those SLAs into consideration before committing to service agreements with its customers.

The first step in defining SLAs is to determine what the customers' expectations are. Factors that influence customer expectation are customer characteristics, criticality of the services provided, and the type of interactions between the provider and the consumer. There are many customer characteristics that influence defining SLAs, for example:

- Consumer versus enterprise customers
- Paying versus nonpaying customers
- Regulated industry versus nonregulated industry
- Anonymous versus personally identifiable

Many cloud services offered directly to consumers for non-mission-critical services do not provide SLAs around performance, uptime, and reliability. The terms of services are heavily weighted toward protecting the CSP and offer the services "as is" to consumers. Consumers must accept those terms to participate. At most, the CSPs will promise to apply best efforts to secure the consumer's data and maintain its privacy.

The stronger the SLA, the more it costs to manage and maintain it. Therefore, nonpaying customers are usually offered lower SLAs than paying customers. As the old saying goes, "You get what you pay for." Some cloud services offer free-trial services for customers to try before they buy. Often, these "freemium" services are run on the lowest cost machines and have limited functionality. The goal of the CSP is to spend as little as possible in an effort to let the consumer take the service for a test ride. Once the customer moves to a paid tier, higher service levels apply.

Customers who require services in a regulated industry require much stronger SLAs than those in a nonregulated industry. Health care, banking, insurance, government, retail, and other industries require strong SLAs around performance, uptime, security, privacy, compliance, and more. Customers using services like photo sharing, streaming video, and social media are usually only offered SLAs around privacy.

The amount of personal information and the type of information that a cloud service requires also has a large influence on SLAs. Some cloud services offer functionality to the general public for free and therefore provide no SLAs. Other cloud services may gather personally identifiable information (PII) like biometric data, Social Security numbers, credit card information, and other attributes that are heavily regulated. If PII data is collected, high levels of security and privacy SLAs are required.

The criticality of the service is a key factor in defining SLAs, as well. Social media services are not mission critical. Nobody dies if Twitter is down for 10 minutes. A company delivering a cloud-based point-of-sale (POS) system must deliver extremely high SLAs because the retailer leveraging the POS solution could lose millions of dollars if it cannot ring up sales across all of its stores. Any service involving financial transactions like online banking, mobile payments, and e-commerce will require very high SLAs. The impact of poor service levels for these types of businesses is substantial. Mission-critical services require the highest SLAs.

It is important to note that a CSP can offer different SLAs for different parts of its products. For example, I worked for a start-up that built a Platform as a Service for executing digital incentives across a large network of retailers. There were four distinct parts of the platform: transaction processing, a business-to-consumer (B2C) component, a business-to-business (B2B) component, and application programming interfaces (APIs). Each part of the platform had very different requirements. The transaction processing was the most critical part of the platform. It connected retailer POS systems to our platform in the cloud in real time. When a consumer shopped at a grocery store, the transaction was sent out of the store to our cloud-based redemption engine, which determined if any digital coupons could be applied to the order. It returned its response to the POS in subseconds, and the POS system deducted the digital coupons from the order and generated the receipt. The SLAs for this part of the platform were incredibly high because any delay or outage could cost the retailer substantial losses in revenue and create customer satisfaction problems. The B2C platform also had to handle millions of transactions a day across the globe. The B2B site, on the other hand, serviced fewer than 100 customers a day and was responsible for loading content into the platform. If the site was down, it did not impact the POS system. The only impact was that new offers could not be added and existing offers could not be altered. The impact and performance requirements of the B2B site were much less critical than the transaction processing and therefore the SLA was lower.

Once the customer characteristics have been identified and the criticality of each component of the architecture has been assessed, the next step is to take an inventory of all of the actors involved in both providing and consuming the cloud services. The SLA of every CSP involved in building the cloud solution should be reviewed and a risk assessment should be performed. For example, if the solution is being built on Rackspace, the company should understand Rackspace's SLAs, and its track record performing against those SLAs, and devise a strategy in the event that Rackspace has an outage. If the cloud service is critical, like the transaction processing service of the digital incentive platform described previously, the architecture will need to account for a fail-over plan if the CSP fails. In the case of the digital incentive platform, the approach taken was to invest heavily in building full redundancy of every layer of the architecture across multiple Amazon Web Services (AWS) availability zones. It was the SLAs that drove that design decision. Our customers demanded that level of service, which justified the investment.

SLAs can drive the cloud service model and cloud deployment model decisions. For example, the SLA for the uptime of the transaction processing module of our digital incentive platform was extremely high and the average monthly response time metric for a transaction was so low that using a PaaS solution was out of the question for two reasons. The first reason was that we needed to have control over the database, the application server, and the operating system to maximize performance and could not rely on a PaaS to meet our performance SLAs. The second reason was that if the transaction processing module did not meet the high uptime required by the SLAs, the retailers would likely terminate the contract. To mitigate that risk we could not afford to be at the mercy of a PaaS solution outage. Some companies under those same constraints might choose to go with a private cloud for that same reason. We felt that with multiple availability zones in AWS, we could meet our SLAs even with a dependency on a public IaaS vendor. The end result was that we never missed a transaction during any AWS outage. Had we leveraged a public PaaS like Heroku and been able to meet the performance metrics, we would have missed some transactions because Heroku has had some outages, and when they occurred there would have been nothing we could have done except wait for Heroku to fix its issues. For the B2B application that might be acceptable, but for the transaction processing it would have been a showstopper.

Consumer expectation is a key factor in determining SLAs. There is a drastic difference in consumer expectation between a social media site like Reddit and an enterprise e-mail solution like Gmail. Many social media sites do not even offer any SLAs around performance and availability. At most they will define terms of service and assure users that they will do their best to protect consumers' personal data. Most of the legal language in the terms of service for social media sites is geared more toward protecting the provider than protecting the consumer. For enterprise solutions, it is quite a different story. Enterprises have an expectation that CSPs will provide high-performance SLAs, usually with an uptime of at least 99 percent but usually higher.

Defining SLAs

A company can be both a cloud consumer and a cloud provider. For example, a consumer of an IaaS cloud service provider builds a SaaS solution and becomes a cloud provider for its customers. In this section, the SLAs that are being discussed are for companies that build solutions on public, private, or hybrid clouds, not vendors like AWS, Rackspace, Microsoft, and others that provide IaaS and PaaS solutions.

The following list shows the types of metrics-based SLAs that are common in contracts between cloud providers and enterprise cloud consumers:

- Overall uptime of application/service
- Page-load times

- Transaction processing times
- API response times
- Reporting response times
- Incident resolution times
- Incident notification times

Tracking and reporting on metrics-based SLAs are accomplished through a combination of logging and monitoring. In Chapter 10, we discussed strategies around collecting log information in a central repository and how to make the logging data relevant by using standard formats, naming conventions, and incident codes. Chapter 12, "Monitoring Strategies," will discuss strategies for monitoring and generating SLA metrics and reports as well as other useful information.

From a regulatory, security, and privacy perspective, the following list shows common requirements that enterprise cloud service consumers demand in contracts from the provider of SaaS and PaaS solutions:

- Security and privacy safeguards
- Published incident response plan (incident retainer also requested on occasion)
- Web vulnerability scans and reports
- Published disaster recovery plans
- Safe harbor agreement
- Data ownership declarations
- Backup and recovery processes document
- Source code escrow

Enterprise customers expect monthly reporting of metrics-based SLAs and often request the right to perform their own annual audit to track security and regulatory-related SLAs. In Chapter 7 we discussed the controls and processes around audit controls. A best practice is to create a document that summarizes all of the security, privacy, and regulatory controls that are in place and provide that to customers on request. Included in that document is a list of all certifications from the various past audits, such as SSAE16, HIPAA, and so on. Also be prepared to provide audit reports, web vulnerability scan reports, monthly metrics reports, and any other artifacts that support ongoing compliance with the SLAs contained in contracts with customers.

For the IT tasks required, a company should create a separate work stream with its own roadmap. There is simply too much work involved to build all of this up front. In the name of minimal viable product (MVP), the product team must plan which user stories are the highest priority and incrementally deliver these user stories over time. For example, if it is January and the expectation is that the product will pass a specific audit by November, there is no need to get all of the security and regulatory stories in the first few sprints and sacrifice core business functionality that may attract additional customers.

The IT user stories are a combination of application development and systems administration tasks. The application developers have to build the user stories that come out of the design sessions on topics such as security, data considerations, logging, monitoring, and so forth. Web-based applications need to be secured against web vulnerabilities and critical data elements must be encrypted for security and privacy. A best practice for building secure web applications is to leverage web frameworks and keep those frameworks current. Examples of web frameworks are Django for Python, .NET Framework for Microsoft, Zend Framework for PHP, Ruby on Rails, and Struts for Java. There are many more frameworks that can be used, but the key is to stay current with the version of the chosen framework because as new vulnerabilities arise, these frameworks get patched to address the new vulnerabilities. Using a framework that is many versions behind may not protect against the more recent exploits. Using a framework does not ensure that the web application is secure, but it does enforce a lot of best practices for securing web applications for many known exploits. I once helped a start-up put together a cloud audit strategy. When we ran the web vulnerability scan, the web application had very few vulnerabilities. Being a young start-up, the product team focused very little on security, but because it leveraged a web framework, the company was protected against most of the top exploits.

The operations team plays a huge role in SLA and regulatory management. As we discussed in Chapter 9, centralization, standardization, and automation are keys to securing systems and passing audits. Operations is responsible for a lot of the automation and policy enforcement that goes into SLA management. We will discuss this more in Chapter 14, "Leveraging a DevOps Culture to Deliver Software Faster and More Reliably."

Managing Vendor SLAs

The top cloud service providers promise a wide variety of SLAs. For most well-established IaaS and PaaS providers, uptime SLAs ranged from 99.9 percent to 100 percent. One major PaaS solution, Heroku, does not provide an uptime SLA, which is astounding in this day and age. A review of the top SaaS solutions, like Salesforce.com, Concur, and others, resulted in no published SLAs at all. The lower down the cloud stack we go, the more demand there is for higher SLAs. One reason why public PaaS solutions are struggling to convince enterprises to use their services is because their SLAs do not meet enterprise standards. This is also why there is a huge increase in interest recently for private PaaS solutions within the enterprise. Companies are willingly taking on the management of the infrastructure and the PaaS software so that they can manage the SLAs themselves, while providing PaaS capabilities to the development teams for increased speed-to-market.

Even when vendors have published SLAs, the value these SLAs have for the customer is often limited to the customer getting a refund or a credit if a significant outage occurs. Regardless of the amount of that refund, it does nothing to repair the collateral damage that the outage may have caused to the business and its customers. This is precisely why so many pundits declare that cloud SLAs are useless. For example, Amazon, Google, Microsoft, and Force.com all have had their outages. Some consumers have survived these outages and some have gone down along with their vendor. When the vendor has a service disruption that disrupts the consumer's services, too, usually the customer is too locked into the cloud service to do anything other than get compensated for the disruption—if they can even get that. For critical applications, make sure the vendor has a good track record living up to its SLAs. This dependency on cloud service providers and their SLAs is unsettling to many companies and their default reaction is often to build their own private clouds. However, most cloud service providers can provide equivalent or better service levels than many individual consumers can provide for themselves.

Before writing off public clouds or hosted private clouds because of concerns with cloud vendors' SLAs, consider the trade-offs. The core competency of companies like Amazon, Rackspace, and Terremark is running data centers. They have invested millions of dollars and have some of the best people in the world working on these data centers. By choosing to build their own private cloud on their own data centers to satisfy the desire to have more control, consumers are betting that they can provide higher SLAs than the cloud providers. In exchange, they give up much of the benefits of cloud computing, such as rapid elasticity, speed-to-market, reduction of capital expenses, and more. Certain companies have a business case or a set of priorities that may justify it, but some companies simply default to private clouds out of personal preference rather than what's best for the business.

What is important to understand about SLAs is that these service levels only represent the uptime of the infrastructure (for IaaS) or the platform (for PaaS); it is up to the engineering teams to build highly available applications on top of them. In the case of AWS, if a company only leverages one zone, the best it can hope for is a 99.95 percent SLA because that is all AWS offers. However, companies can achieve much greater SLAs on AWS if they architect across zone or across region redundancy.

An interesting fact is that many of the major SaaS players get away without publishing SLAs. My theory is that a lot of them were early pioneers in this space and built up a large installed base before many customers started to demand high SLAs in the request-for-proposal (RFP) process. It would be very hard for a new SaaS company selling cloud services into enterprises to have much success without establishing SLAs. Many would never get a shot at an RFP because consumers are starting to demand more security and SLAs from their cloud providers. For companies building mission-critical SaaS solutions today, it should be expected that customers will be requiring an SLA of at least 99.9 percent. The more mission critical the service, the higher the customer expectation will be for that number.

All of the major cloud vendors, whether they are IaaS, PaaS, or SaaS, have made it a priority to become compliant with most of the major regulations, such as SSAE 16, SAS 70, HIPAA, ISO, PCI, and others, that are applicable to the services being provided. Most vendors would never be considered by enterprise customers if they did not have these certifications posted on their websites. Most enterprises must comply with these same regulations and to accomplish that the vendor solutions they choose must also comply with the same regulations or be exempt from those regulations.

AES CASE STUDY: **Service Level Agreements**

Acme eAuctions (AEA) had never published SLAs before because it had a closed, proprietary auction site. The new site will be a PaaS that third parties build solutions on. In order to attract customers willing to pay transaction fees for executing auctions and provide applications in the App Store, AEA will have to guarantee service levels. After discussing SLAs with the product team, AEA decided to divide the system up into components and provide SLAs for each component.

- Seller services—9.9 percent uptime, recovery time of one day
- Buyer services—99.9 percent uptime, recovery time of 15 minutes
- API layer—99.9 percent uptime, performance guarantee of one second or less, recovery time 15 minutes
- App Store—99.percent uptime, recovery time seven days
- Published privacy policy

Here is how the team arrived at these numbers. First, it recognized that different components have different uptime and performance requirements because of their impact. For example, nothing is more critical than processing auctions, which is why the buyer services have the strictest SLAs. The API layer provides access to buyer services, so it aligns with buyer services and has an added performance requirement of one second that many of the company's potential customers were requiring in their contracts. The seller services are important but not quite as critical as the buyer services. When the seller services are down or not performing, it impacts adding new content to the site, but existing auctions can still occur. The App Store is where developers can add applications to assist buyers and sellers with a variety of tools. Even though it generates some revenue, it is not mission critical, so a lower SLA and recovery time are provided.

Terms and conditions are published on the website and consumers agree to those terms when the sign up. For third-party partners, AEA has an online agreement of terms that they must sign. However, large, influential customers, like a large electronics manufacturer, may require more stringent SLAs. PCI DSS is out of scope since AEA is off-loading payments and seller fees to third parties. However, it is possible that a large customer may require a security audit such as an SSAE 16 or SOC2 audit. Until someone asks for it, there is no need to add it, especially with a looming due date.

Summary

SLAs are a pledge from a service provider to a service consumer that specific performance metrics will be met, a certain level of security and privacy will be upheld, and if required, the provider has been certified for specific regulations. The more mission critical the service being provided, the more SLAs the cloud service provider will be required to deliver to the cloud service consumer. Cloud services targeting enterprise customers will usually have strict SLA requirements, while cloud services targeting consumers will usually provide basic terms of service that protect the cloud service provider more than the cloud service consumer.

References

Greer, M. (2012, April 10). "Practical Guide to Cloud Service Level Agreements." Retrieved from   http://www.cloudstandardscustomercouncil.org/PGCloudSLA040512MGreer .pdf.

Diaz, A. (2011, December 14). "Service Level Agreements in the Cloud: Who Cares?" Retrieved from http://www.wired.com/insights/2011/12/service-level-agreements-in-the-cloud-who-cares/.

Myerson, J. (2013, January 7). "Best Practices to Develop SLAs for Cloud Computing." Retrieved from http://www.ibm.com/developerworks/cloud/library/cl-slastandards/.

CHAPTER 12

Monitoring Strategies

Real-time monitoring is the new face of testing.

—Noah Sussman

Most cloud services are built to be always on, meaning the customer expects to be able to use the service 24 hours a day, 365 days a year. A considerable amount of engineering is required to build cloud services that provide the high levels of uptime, reliability, and scalability required to be always on. Even with a great architecture, it still takes a proactive monitoring strategy in order to meet the service level agreements (SLAs) required to deliver a system that does not go down. This chapter discusses strategies for monitoring cloud services.

Proactive vs. Reactive Monitoring

Many IT shops are accustomed to monitoring systems to detect failures. These shops track the consumption of memory, CPU, and disk space of servers and the throughput of the network to detect symptoms of system failures. Tools that ping URLs to check if websites are responding are very common, as well. All of these types of monitors are reactive. The tools tell us either that something is failing or that something is about to fail. Reactive monitoring focuses on detection. There should be a corresponding monitoring strategy for prevention.

The goal of proactive monitoring is to prevent failures. Prevention requires a different mind-set than detection. To prevent failures, we first must define what healthy system metrics look like. Once we define the baseline metrics for a healthy system, we must watch patterns to detect when data is trending toward an unhealthy system and fix the problem before our reactive monitors start sounding the warning bells. Combining both reactive and proactive monitoring is a best practice for implementing cloud services that must always be on. Proactive or preventive monitoring strives to find and resolve issues early, before they have a large impact on the overall system and to increase the odds that the issues are found and corrected before the customer is impacted.

What Needs to Be Monitored?

The purpose of monitoring is to help track that systems are behaving in-line with their expectations. Back in Chapter 11, "SLA Management," we discussed that SLAs set an expectation between the cloud service provider and the cloud service consumer regarding the level of service that will be provided. To ensure that these SLAs are met, each SLA must be monitored, measured, and reported on. There are metrics-based SLAs such as response time and uptime, and there are SLAs focusing on processes around privacy, security, and regulations. Monitoring should cover all types of SLAs.

But SLAs are only part of the story. Many cloud-based services are distributed systems composed of many parts. All parts of the system are a point of failure and need to be monitored. Different people within the organization may need different information about the system in order to ensure that the system functions properly. For example, a front-end developer might be concerned with page-load times, network performance, the performance of the application programming interfaces (APIs), and so forth. The database architects may want to see metrics about the database server in the areas of threads, cache, memory, and CPU utilization in addition to metrics about the SQL statements and their response times. The system administrators may want to see metrics such as requests per second (RPS), disk space capacity, and CPU and memory utilization. The product owners may want to see how many unique visits per day, new users, cost per user, and other business-related metrics.

All of these metrics provide insights to determine if the system is behaving correctly and if the system is causing the desired behaviors from the end users. A system can be running flawlessly from a technology standpoint, but if the customer usage is consistently declining, there might be something drastically wrong in the areas of usability or product strategy. Metrics are also critical for accessing the success of each deployment. When a new version of software is deployed, it is critical to watch key system metrics and compare them against the baseline to see if the deployment has a negative impact on the overall system. For systems that use switches to turn features on and off, tracking metrics post-deployment can help discover when a switch is inadvertently set to the wrong value. This preventive measure can allow for a mistake to be quickly fixed before the error becomes problematic. Without a preventive approach, a simple issue like an erroneous configuration setting might not be found until a long time later, when reporting data shows a large delta in the data or, even worse, by the customers discovering it first.

A number of categories should be monitored:

- Performance
- Throughput
- Quality
- Key performance indicators (KPIs)
- Security
- Compliance

Monitoring also occurs within the different layers of the cloud stack:

- User layer
- Application layer
- Application stack layer
- Infrastructure layer

In addition, there are three distinct domains that need to be monitored:

1. Cloud vendor environment
2. Cloud application environment
3. User experience

Let's briefly touch on each one of these areas. The intent of this chapter is to give a broad overview of some basic metrics and best practices. For a more in-depth commentary on measuring metrics for scaling systems, I recommend Cal Henderson's book, *Building Scalable Websites*, in which he explains how the team at Flickr scaled out the company's famous photo-sharing website.

Monitoring Strategies by Category

There are many categories of information that can be monitored. In this chapter, we will discuss monitoring strategies for measuring performance, throughput, quality, KPIs, security, and compliance. Each company will have a unique set of categories that are relevant to its business model and the target application. The categories discussed here are the ones that are typical in any cloud application or service.

Performance

Performance is an important metric within each layer of the cloud stack. At the user layer, performance metrics track attributes about how the users interact with the system. Here are some examples of user performance metrics:

- Number of new customers
- Number of unique visitors per day
- Number of page visits per day
- Average time spend on site
- Revenue per customer
- Bounce rate (percent of users who leave without viewing pages)
- Conversion rate (percent of users who perform desired action based on direct marketing)

The goal of these metrics is to measure the behavior of the customers using the system. If these numbers decrease drastically from the baseline numbers after a deployment, there is a good chance either that there is an issue with the new code or that the new features were not well received by the customers.

Sometimes the end user is not a person but another system. Similar metrics can be used to ensure that the system and its users are behaving in the expected manner.

- Number of new users
- Number of unique users per day
- Number of calls per user per day
- Average time per call
- Revenue per user

In this case a user represents another system. If the expectation is that the number of users is fixed or static and the metric shows the number is decreasing, then there is likely a problem preventing the system from getting access or the requests are failing. If the number of users goes up, then there might be a security issue and unauthorized accounts are gaining access. If the number of users is dynamic, then a decline in any of the metrics might be evidence that there are issues with the system.

At the application layer, performance measures how the system responds to the end user, whether that user is a person or another system. Here are some common performance metrics that are often tracked:

- Page-load times
- Uptime
- Response time (APIs, reports, queries, etc.)

These metrics might be tracked and aggregated at different levels. For example, a system may be made up of a consumer-facing web page, a collection of APIs, an administrator portal for data management, and a reporting subsystem. It would be wise to track these metrics for each one of the four components separately because they likely all have unique performance requirements and SLAs. Also, if this system is being delivered as a Software as a Service (SaaS) solution to numerous clients, it would be wise to track these metrics uniquely by client, as well.

At the application stack layer, the metrics are similar, but instead of tracking the application performance, now we are tracking the performance of the underlying components of the application stack, such as the operating system, application server, database server, caching layer, and so on. Every component that makes up this layer needs to be monitored on every machine. If a MySQL database is made up of a master node with three slave nodes, each node needs to have a baseline established and needs to be tracked against its baseline. The same applies for the web servers. A 100-node web server farm needs each node to be monitored independently. At the same time, servers need to be monitored in clusters or groups to compute the metrics for a given customer. For example, if each customer has its own dedicated master and slave databases, the average response time and uptime is the aggregation of performance metrics for all of the servers in the cluster.

At the infrastructure layer, the metrics apply to the physical infrastructure, such as servers, networks, routers, and so on. Public Infrastructure as a Service (IaaS) providers will host a web page showing the health of their infrastructure, but they only give red, yellow, and green indicators, which indicate whether the services are functioning normally, are having issues, or are completely down.

Throughput

Throughput measures average rate at which data moves through the system. Like performance, it is important to understand the throughput at each layer of the cloud stack, at each component of the system, and for each unique customer. At the user layer, throughput measures how many concurrent users or sessions the system is processing. At the application layer, throughput measures how much data the system can transmit from the application stack layer through the application layer to the end user. This metric is often measured in transactions per second (TPS), RPS, or some business-related metric like click-throughs per second, requests per second (RPS), or page visits per second.

At the application stack layer, measuring throughput is critical in diagnosing issues within the system. If the TPS at the application layer is lower than normal, it is usually due to a reduction in throughput to one or many components within the application stack. Common monitoring solutions like open source Nagios or SaaS products like New Relic are commonly used to gather various metrics on the application stack components. These tools allow the administrators to set alerts and notifications when certain thresholds are met and provide analytics for spotting trends in the data. At the infrastructure layer, throughput measures the flow from physical servers and other hardware and network devices.

Quality

Quality is a measure of both the accuracy of information and impact of defects on the end user in the production environment. The key here is the emphasis on the production environment. Having 1,000 defects in the quality assurance or development environments is meaningless to an end user and to the SLAs of a system. It is the number of defects and the impacts they have on the applications and the end users that matter. One hundred defects in production might sound horrible, but if a majority of them have no or minimal impact on the end user, then they have less impact on the measurement of quality. I bring this up because I have seen too many companies use a quality metric to drive the wrong results. Quality should not be measured in bugs or defects. If it is, the team spends valuable time correcting many defects that do not have an impact on the overall health of the system and the end user's perception. Instead, quality should focus on accuracy, the correctness of the data that is being returned to the end user; the error rates, the frequency in which errors occur; deployment failure rates, the percentage of time deployments fail or have issues; and customer satisfaction, the perception of quality and service from the voice of the customer.

To measure quality, standardization of data collection is required. As was mentioned in Chapter 10, error codes, severity level, and log record formats should all be standardized and common error and logging APIs should be used to ensure that consistent data is sent to the central logging system. Automated reports and dashboards that mine the data from the logging system should generate all of the relevant key metrics, including quality, error rates, error types, and so forth. Thresholds should be set that cause alerts and notifications to be triggered when the quality metric reaches the alert threshold. Quality must be maintained at every layer within the cloud stack.

At the user layer, quality measures the success and accuracy of user registration and access. If an unacceptable number of users fail the registration process, somebody must resolve the issue quickly. Sometimes the quality issue is not a defect but rather a usability issue. Users may require more training or the user interface may be too cumbersome or confusing. At the application layer, quality is in the eye of the beholder, also known as the end user. At this layer we are concerned with the defect types. Errors related to erroneous data, failed transactions, and 400- to 500-level http response codes are typically the culprits that cause invalid results and unhappy customers. These errors must be tracked for each API and for each module within the system. At the application stack layer, errors need to be logged and tracked for each component and the same applies to the physical infrastructure within the infrastructure layer.

KPIs

Key performance indicators are those metrics that tell us if the system is meeting the business goals. Some examples of KPIs are:

- Revenue per customer
- Revenue per hour
- Number of incoming customer calls per day
- Number of jobs completed per day
- Site traffic
- Shopping cart abandonment rate

KPIs are unique to each company's business model. Each company invests in systems to achieve its business goals. Monitoring and measuring KPIs is a best practice for proactively detecting potential issues. Detecting KPIs trending in the wrong direction allows the team to proactively research root causes and potentially fix the issue(s) before too much damage is done. It is also important to detect when KPIs are trending in a positive direction so the team can figure out what the catalyst is so the team can understand what drives the appropriate behaviors.

KPIs are measured at the application layer. Typically, the product team establishes what those key metrics are. IT teams often establish their own KPIs, as well. In Chapter 14, we will discuss how metrics are used to proactively monitor the health of the underlying architecture and deployment processes.

Security

Securing cloud-based systems can be quite a challenge. The methods that cyber-criminals and other people or systems that attack systems with malicious intent deploy are very dynamic. A system that is very secure today can be exposed tomorrow as new and more complex threats are launched. To combat the dynamic nature of security threats, a system should proactively monitor all components for suspicious patterns. There are many good books that go into great detail about securing systems, and I'll spare you the gory details. The point to get across in this book is that building security into a system is only part of the job. In Chapter 9, we discussed the PDP method, which stands for *protection*, *detection*, and *prevention*. Monitoring is one area where detection and protection take place. Monitoring security is a proactive approach that focuses on mining log files and discovering abnormal patterns that have the potential of being an unsuccessful or successful attempt at attacking the system.

As with the other metrics discussed in this chapter, security should be monitored at every layer of the cloud stack and at every component within each layer. Every component of a system typically requires some level of authentication in order for a user or a system to access it. Security monitoring should look at all failed authentication attempts for every component and detect if there is a certain user, system, or IP address that is constantly trying and failing to authenticate. Most attacks are attempted by unattended scripts, usually referred to as *bots*. These bots work their way into the system through some unsecure component and then run a series of other scripts that try to access any application or server that it can.

Once detected, administrators can blacklist the IP address to prevent it from doing any damage. The next step is prevention. How did the intruder gain access in the first place? Without detection, the only way to know that an outside threat has penetrated the system is when the threat accomplishes its objectives, which could be catastrophic, such as stealing sensitive data, destroying or corrupting files and systems, installing viruses and worms, consuming compute resources that impact the system performance, and many other horrible scenarios. For systems that are required to pass security audits, it is mandatory to implement a PDP security strategy.

Compliance

Systems that fall under various regulatory constraints should implement a monitoring strategy for compliance. The goal of this strategy is to raise alerts when parts of the system are falling out of compliance. Compliance requires policies and procedures to be followed both within a system and within the business. Examples of policies that the business must follow are policies pertaining to running background checks on employees and restricting access to buildings. Policies pertaining to the system, such as restricting production access on a need-to-know basis, can be monitored within the system. Once again, a team can mine log files to track enforcement of policies. There are also many new SaaS and open source tools that have recently entered the marketplace that allow policies to be set up in the tools, and then the tools monitor the enforcement of these policies. These tools raise alerts and offer canned and ad hoc reporting for monitoring policy enforcement.

Monitoring is not a silver bullet. But without information and tools, systems are ticking time bombs waiting to go off at any minute. Monitoring allows people to learn about their systems. The best and most reliable systems are ones that are always changing and adapting to the environment around them. Whether it is tweaks to the code, the infrastructure, the product, or the customer experience, it takes insights provided by information to make the right changes in order to create the desired result. Without monitoring, a system is like a fish out of water.

Monitoring by Cloud Service Level

Now that we know what to monitor, let's see how monitoring is accomplished within each cloud service model. As with everything else in the cloud, the further down the cloud stack you go, the more responsibility you take on. Starting with SaaS, there is very little, if anything, that the end user needs to do. The SaaS service is either up or down. If it is down or appears to be down, most SaaS solutions have a web page that shows the latest status, and they have a customer support web page and phone number to call. If the SaaS system is critical to the business, then the end user may want some kind of alert to be triggered when the service is down. Some SaaS vendors have a feature that allows end users to get alerts. If the SaaS tool does not have this feature, the end user can use a tool like Pingdom that pings the URL and alerts the appropriate people that the service is unavailable. Even with this alerting capability, with SaaS there is nothing the end user can do but wait until the vendor restores the service.

In Chapter 13, "Disaster Recovery Planning," we will discuss the idea of having a secondary SaaS solution in place in case the primary service goes down. For example, if an e-commerce site leverages a SaaS solution for processing online payments or for fulfillment and the service goes down, the e-commerce site could detect the failure and configure itself to switch over to its secondary provider until the service is recovered. The trigger for this event could be an alert message from the URL monitoring software.

Public and private Platform as a Service (PaaS) solutions handle monitoring differently. With public PaaS, the vendor manages both the infrastructure layer and the application stack layer. The PaaS vendor supplies APIs to various monitoring and logging solutions that they integrate with. The application code that the consumer builds on top of the PaaS should leverage these APIs so that all logs go to the PaaS-provided central logging system (if that is desirable). The consumer can use its own monitoring tools or it can leverage the APIs of the monitoring tools that are integrated with the PaaS. Not all PaaS solutions have intrusion detection tools that are exposed to the end user. The thought process here is that the vendor owns that responsibility and the consumer should focus on its applications.

Private PaaS is more like IaaS. For both, the consumer must monitor the system down to the application stack layer. Like public PaaS, many private PaaS solutions have plug-ins for modern logging and monitoring solutions. For IaaS solutions, the logging and monitoring solutions must be installed and managed by the consumer. For companies building their own private clouds, they must also monitor the physical infrastructure and data center.

AEA CASE STUDY: **Monitoring Considerations**

The Acme eAuctions (AEA) auction platform is made up of many components that support many actors. There are many points of failure that need to be monitored. Uptime, performance, reliability, security, and scalability are all important to the success of the platform. AEA will want to proactively monitor the platform to minimize any service interruptions, performance degradation, or security breaches. In order to protect the platform from the misuse of resources (intentional or unintentional) by the external partners, the partners' resources will be throttled at predefined maximum levels. Here is a short list of items that AEA determined that it must monitor:

- Infrastructure—memory, disk, CPU utilization, bandwidth, and so on
- Database—query performance, memory, caching, throughput, swap space, and the like
- Application—transactions per second, page-load times, API response time, availability, and so forth
- Access—external partner resource consumption
- Security—repeated failed login attempts, unauthorized access
- KPIs—financial metrics, transaction metrics, performance metrics
- Costs—cloud cost optimization

AEA will need to use a variety of monitoring tools to satisfy these requirements. Some of these tools will mine the centralized log files to raise alerts, such as detecting repeated login failures from a single intrusion detection. There are both open source and commercial tools for monitoring infrastructure and databases. There are some great SaaS solutions, like New Relic, that can be configured to set performance, availability, and service level thresholds and alert the appropriate people when those metrics fall out of range. Another important tool is the *cloud cost monitoring* solution. It is easy to quickly provision cloud resources. The downside is that it is easy to run up the monthly infrastructure bill just as fast if a close eye is not kept on the costs.

Understanding your monitoring requirements up front allows you to find monitoring solutions that can meet many of your overall needs. Companies that don't take an enterprise approach to evaluating their monitoring needs often wind up with too many different tools, which makes it hard to piece together data from various unrelated systems. By looking across the enterprise, monitoring requirements can be satisfied by fewer tools and hopefully by tools that can be integrated with each other.

Summary

Monitoring is a critical component of any cloud-based system. A monitoring strategy should be put in place early on and continuously improved over time. There is no one monitoring tool that will meet all the needs of a cloud solution. Expect to leverage a combination of SaaS and open source solutions and possibly even some homegrown solutions to meet the entire needs of the platform. Managing a cloud solution without a monitoring strategy is like driving down the highway at night with the lights off. You might make it home safe, but you might not!

Reference

Henderson, C. (2006). *Building Scalable Websites*. Cambridge, MA. O'Reilly.

CHAPTER 13

Disaster Recovery Planning

Every big computing disaster has come from taking too many ideas and putting them in one place.

—GORDON BELL

When it comes to technology, everything can and will fail. In distributed environments, like many cloud-based solutions, there are many moving parts and any part of the system can fail at any time. The secret to surviving failures is to expect everything to fail and design for those failures. Failures come in many forms. The damage caused by a web server crashing is easily mitigated by having multiple web servers behind a load balancer. A database server crashing is a more severe failure that requires more systems thinking to properly recover from. A data center going down is an even more severe failure and can ruin a business if a well-designed disaster recovery solution is not in place.

Each cloud service model has a different set of challenges when it comes to disasters. In the following paragraphs we will discuss some best practices for each cloud service model when dealing with disaster situations in the cloud.

What Is the Cost of Downtime?

Cloud computing allows us to build systems faster and cheaper than ever before. There are countless stories of how companies rapidly built and deployed solutions that would have taken many months or years to deploy in precloud days. But getting a solution to the marketplace is only half of the story. The other half of the story is deploying a solution that can recover from disasters, big or small. When it comes to disaster recovery, it still comes down to good old architecture and planning.

The strategies for disaster recovery for cloud solutions are fundamentally the same as the strategies we have had in place for our data centers for years and years. The implementation may be different but the way we go about system design is the same. The first step in the process is to understand three important variables from a business perspective. The first variable is the recovery time objective (RTO) or the time within which the business requires that the service is back up and running. For example, a company running a high-traffic e-commerce site might lose thousands of dollars per minute when customers cannot order goods. The RTO for the e-commerce site might be five minutes or less. That same company might have a reporting system that could tolerate being down for a longer period of time because the reports do not have as much impact on revenue or customer satisfaction. The RTO for the reports might be several days or even up to a week if a disaster were to occur.

The second variable is the recovery point objective (RPO) or the amount of time in which data loss can be tolerated. Using the e-commerce example, the parts of the system that handle financial transactions most likely have zero or near-zero tolerance for losing any data. If the e-commerce application has a social feature where buyers can share thoughts about the products across their social networks, the company can tolerate a longer period of time where data may be lost.

The third variable is value, which is a measurement of how much it is worth to the company to mitigate disaster situations. There are many factors that may influence the value that a company puts on recovery. Here are a few examples.

The customers of a cloud service can greatly influence the value of recovery. For example, when our digital incentive platform first launched, our first customer was a small family-owned grocery chain. At that point in time we had what we called "good enough" recovery whereby, if a disaster occurred, we could be running in another availability zone in an hour or two. The process to recover was not automated at that time. Once we started engaging with the top retailers, it was apparent that we needed real-time recovery from any disaster that drove our investments to build fully redundant virtual data centers across multiple availability zones. Our customers drove up the value of recovery because of the potential for revenue and market share that would result in successfully serving the biggest retailers.

Another example is the criticality of the service. There are a number of factors that make a service critical. If the service is critical to the lives of patients or the safety of citizens, then the value of recovery is likely very high. Public perception is another factor that can drive the criticality. For example, there are a number of companies competing for market share in the Internet music space. Pandora, Last.fm, and Spotify are just a few of them. If one of them were perceived as being more unreliable than the others because of its inability to quickly recover from outages, it would be extremely challenging to compete.

The business should determine the RTO, RPO, and the value of recovery for each functional area of the architecture. These values should drive the investments that IT makes in order to provide the right level of recovery for each functional area. The next section will discuss disaster recovery strategies for each cloud service model.

Disaster Recovery Strategies for IaaS

Infrastructure as a Service (IaaS) disaster recovery strategies are much more involved than Platform as a Service (PaaS) and Software as a Service (SaaS), because the cloud service consumer (CSC) is responsible for the application stack. With public IaaS solutions the CSC is dependent on the cloud service provider (CSP) for managing the physical data center. This chapter will focus on how to recover if any layer within the cloud stack is in a disaster situation but will not discuss strategies for operating physical data centers.

Public IaaS cloud providers like Amazon and Rackspace have had their share of outages over the years. It would be foolish to expect otherwise. There are many ways to design in anticipation of these failures. Let's start with some examples of preventing disasters when Amazon has outages.

Amazon has regions and availability zones. The regions are located across the globe while the zones are independent virtual data centers within a region. For example, the U.S.-East region located in the Virginia data center has four zones (a, b, c, and d). Historically, Amazon Web Services (AWS) outages have occurred in a single availability zone. Smart companies that have built redundancy across multiple zones have been able to maintain uptime even when AWS has outages (we will discuss how to build redundancy later in the chapter). However, sometimes an applications programming interface (API) has an outage that can impact multiple zones. For example, Amazon Elastic Block Store (EBS) is a service that provides network-attached disks, which is usually where the database is installed. If the EBS has issues across zones, cross-zone redundancy would not prevent the system from failing.

One method to combat this issue on AWS is build redundancy across regions. Cross-region redundancy is more complex and expensive than cross-zone redundancy. Moving data across zones incurs charges for the data transfer and introduces latency that does not exist between availability zones within a region. The cost and complexity of cross-region redundancy needs to be balanced with the value of recovery, RTO, and RPO established by the business.

Another method is to implement a hybrid cloud solution. With Amazon, this can be accomplished by leveraging a private cloud vendor that supports Amazon's APIs. Eucalyptus is a company that provides AWS-compatible APIs, but it is important to note that they only support a subset of the APIs that

AWS offers to its customers. For an AWS-Eucalyptus hybrid approach, architects would be wise to restrict their AWS API usage to just those APIs that are supported on the Eucalyptus platform if they want all parts of the system to be recoverable. Using Eucalyptus in a hybrid cloud approach is essentially creating another availability zone, except that the APIs in this private zone are isolated from any issues that may occur on AWS.

Rackspace provides both public and private IaaS functionality. It is possible to create a hybrid cloud solution leveraging open source cloud software like Open Stack and running the exact same cloud software on both the public and private cloud. In fact, the private cloud could be located in any data center, whether it is at Rackspace, the company's own data center, or some other hosted facility.

Another approach is to leverage multiple public cloud vendors. To do this effectively, the systems must be built in a way that does not lock you into the IaaS vendor. This is easier said than done. For example, one of the huge benefits of AWS and other IaaS providers is the large selection of APIs that can be leveraged to quickly build applications and focus more on solving business problems. To be *cloud agnostic*, one must refrain from using these proprietary APIs, thus devaluing the vendor offering. Another approach is to isolate the areas in the code that call the IaaS APIs and have logic that detects which IaaS vendor to leverage and then execute the appropriate API. The best way to accomplish the goal of leveraging multiple public cloud vendors is to leverage an open source cloud solution like Open Stack across both public IaaS providers.

Many companies feel that building redundancy across AWS availability zones is a sufficient disaster recovery strategy. Unless the value of recovery is extremely high, I would agree, given that historically, AWS outages have been isolated to single zones. However, it is important to know that even though an AWS region has multiple zones, all zones are still in the same general location. For example, all U.S.-East zones are in Virginia. If there were a major catastrophic event in Virginia, there is the potential that all U.S.-East zones could go down. The next section describes four different approaches for dealing with disasters where either the database is unavailable or the entire data center is unavailable. These approaches can be applied to public, private, or hybrid cloud solutions and also to AWS regions or zones.

Recovering from a Disaster in the Primary Data Center

Whether you are using public, private, or hybrid IaaS solutions, there is a standard set of best practices for recovering the database in the unfortunate event that the database or the data center is in a disaster state. Following are four common methods of recovery for leveraging a secondary data center (physical or virtual) to protect against disasters within the primary data center:

1. Classic backup and restore method
2. Redundant data centers—Active-Passive Cold
3. Redundant data centers—Active-Passive Warm
4. Redundant data centers—Active-Active Hot

Classic Backup and Restore Method

In this method (see Figure 13.1), daily full backups and incremental backups are created during the day and stored to a disk service provided by the cloud vendor. The backups are also copied to the secondary data center and possibly to some other third-party vendor just to be extra safe.

If the database goes off-line, gets corrupted, or encounters some other issue, we can restore the last good backup and apply the latest incremental backups on top of that. If those are unavailable, we can go to the secondary site and pull the last good full backup and the incremental backups dated after the full backup.

This method is the cheapest solution because there are no redundant servers running. The downside of this approach is that the RTO is very long

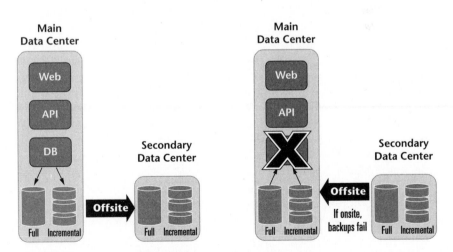

Figure 13.1   Classic Backup and Recovery Method

because the database cannot be brought back online until all of the relevant backups have been restored and the data quality has been verified. This method has been used for years in our brick-and-mortar data centers.

Active-Passive Cold

In this model (see Figure 13.2), the secondary data center is prepared to take over the duties from the primary data center if the primary is in a disaster state. The term *cold* means that the redundant servers are not on and running. Instead, a set of scripts is ready to be executed in case of an emergency, which will provision a set of servers that is configured exactly the same as the resources that run at the primary data center. When a disaster has been declared, the team runs these automated scripts that create database servers and restore the latest backups. It also provisions all of the other servers (web servers, application servers, etc.) and essentially establishes a duplicated environment in a secondary data center, hence the term *cold*. This method is a cost-effective way to deal with outages because the cold servers do not cost anything until they are provisioned; however, if the RTO for an outage is less than a few minutes, it will not be an acceptable plan. Restoring databases from tape or disk is a time-consuming task that could take several minutes to several hours, depending on the size of the database. The Active-Passive Cold approach is for high-RTO recoveries.

Active-Passive Warm

The warm method (see Figure 13.3) runs the database server *hot*, meaning that it is always on and always in sync with the master data center. The other servers are cold or off and are only provisioned when the disaster recovery plan is executed. This method costs more than the Active-Passive Cold method, because the hot database servers are always on and running, but greatly reduces the amount of downtime if an outage occurred because no database restore would be required. The recovery time would be the time it takes to provision all of the nondatabase servers, which can usually be accomplished in a few minutes if the process is scripted. Another advantage of this approach is that the hot database at the secondary data center can be allocated for use as opposed to sitting idle, waiting for a disaster to be declared. For example, ad hoc and business intelligence workloads could be pointed to this secondary data center's database instances segregating reporting workloads from online transaction processing workloads, thus improving the overall efficiency of the master database.

For systems with a low RPO, running a live and in-sync database at a secondary data center is a great way to reduce the loss of data while speeding up the time to recovery.

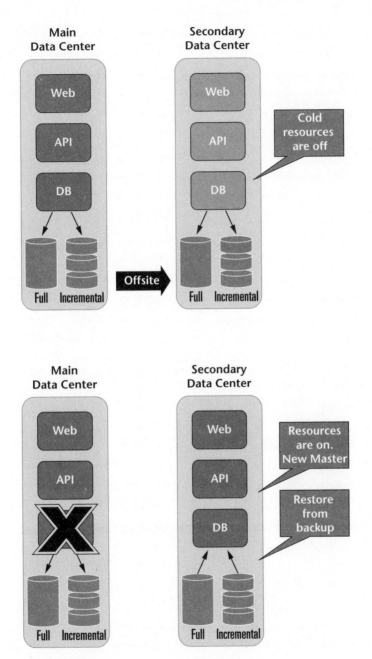

Figure 13.2 Redundant Data Centers—Active-Passive Cold

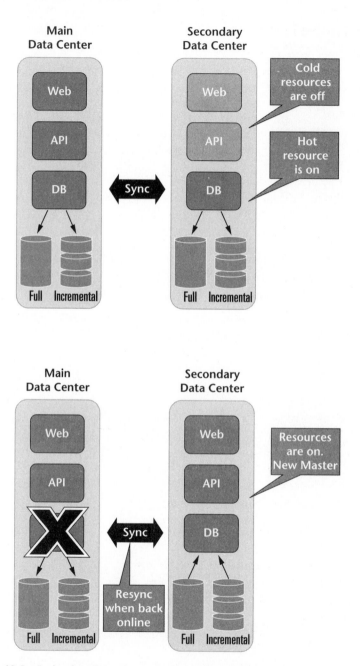

Figure 13.3 Redundant Data Centers—Active-Passive Warm

Active-Active Hot

The most expensive but most resilient method is to run fully redundant data centers at all times (see Figure 13.4). The beauty of this model is that all of the compute resources are being used at all times and in many cases a complete failure of one data center may not cause any downtime at all. This is the model that we used for the digital incentives platform. That platform has survived every AWS outage without ever missing a transaction, while many major websites were down. We had a low tolerance for lost data and downtime, and the value of recovery to the business was extremely high because of the risk of impacting our customers' point-of-sale systems.

In this model, the database uses master–slave replication across data centers. When the primary data center fails, the database at the secondary data center becomes the new master. When the failed data center recovers, the databases that were down start to sync up. Once all data in all data centers is back in sync, control can be given back to the primary data center to become the master again. Active-Active Hot is the way to go when the value of recovery is extremely high and failure is not an option.

Disaster Recovery Strategies for PaaS

With public PaaS, the entire platform, which includes the application stack and the infrastructure, is the responsibility of the vendor and the consumer is responsible for the applications built on top of the platform. The promise of public PaaS is to abstract away all of the work required to handle the underlying infrastructure and application stack, including scaling databases, designing for fail over, patching servers, and much more, so developers can focus on business requirements. That downside of public PaaS is that when a disaster occurs, the consumer is at the mercy of the PaaS provider's disaster recovery plan. For mission-critical applications, it is a tough pill to swallow to have no control over when the applications will be back up again. There have been occasions where AWS has had issues in an availability zone that have caused outages in public PaaS providers like Heroku. When this happened many developers flocked to forums and blogs to voice their frustration as their applications remained down and they could do nothing about it.

If reliance on a public PaaS for disaster recovery is too risky for a company, private PaaS providers are a great alternative. With private PaaS, the vendor abstracts the development platform so installing and managing the application stack becomes simple and automated, but the consumer now has to manage the infrastructure. That may sound unfortunate, but when a disaster occurs, the consumer is back in control of the situation since it manages the physical or virtual infrastructure.

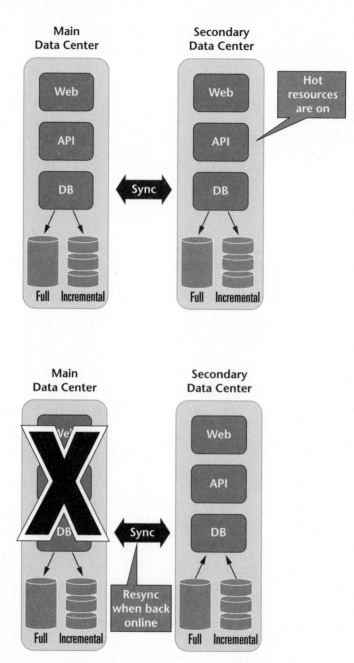

Figure 13.4   Redundant Data Centers—Active-Active Hot

In fact, the best disaster recovery strategy for a public PaaS is to leverage a PaaS provider that allows the PaaS platform to be run in any data center whether it is on-premises or in the public cloud. Open source solutions like Red Hat's OpenShift and Cloud Foundry offer hybrid cloud solutions. Consumers can install these PaaS solutions on a public IaaS like AWS or Rackspace and locally in their own data center. Both the public IaaS data center and the private IaaS data center can run various workloads and act as secondary data centers if the primary fails. These four methods of recovery can be applied in a private or hybrid PaaS scenario.

Disaster Recovery Strategies for SaaS

We have discussed strategies for escaping outages in the cloud for PaaS and IaaS. Sometimes these outages are caused by the cloud service providers themselves, and sometimes there are true disasters related to weather, terrorism, or other catastrophic events. But what about SaaS? Many consumers don't consider any strategies for SaaS solutions, which could lead to serious business impacts if a disaster were to occur. How many companies actually have a disaster recovery plan for the use case where Salesforce.com is unavailable for an extended period of time? What would a company do if its SaaS-based financial system went off-line for a week? It would not be pretty. For SaaS solutions, if the data or business processes are mission critical, there had better be a plan for operating if the service is not available. Minimally, the SaaS contract from the vendor should have a software escrow. A SaaS software escrow protects the buyer if the SaaS vendor goes out of business or is purchased by another company and severs the existing contract. The escrow holds the vendor's IP in an independent third party's holding area where it may be released to the buyer if the vendor goes out of business or kills the product. This essentially gives the buyer the ownership of the data.

Escrows are great for protecting your rights and ownership, but they don't do much for getting your business back up and running. Businesses should document and practice manual processes as a plan to combat a major outage for any mission-critical SaaS functionality. In some cases, it may even be feasible to use two different SaaS vendors to protect against outages. For example, let's say that a business is running an e-commerce site that generates $1 million a day in online sales. Instead of reinventing the wheel it decides to leverage a best-in-breed shopping cart and credit card processing SaaS solution. If this SaaS solution fails, the company risks losing $700 a minute. It would be wise for the company to use a second SaaS solution, either in a round-robin fashion or as a hot backup. Most of these solutions charge by transaction, so a hot backup method would not be an expensive undertaking.

Another disastrous situation is the use case where a cloud vendor goes out of business or is bought by another company and shut down. SaaS consumers should think about requesting data extracts for any SaaS application that is storing critical data. Having the data may not enable the consumer to get a system up and running quickly, but it does prevent data loss and does allow for data to be loaded into a database for querying. Without the data, if the SaaS vendor shuts down, the consumer does not have the ability to do anything other than take a legal action to try to get access to its data or hope that the vendor has enough resources left to provide it with its data. From a risk-mitigation standpoint, it is much safer to get a regularly scheduled extract even if nothing is done with it other than to archive it.

Disaster Recovery Hybrid Clouds

Hybrid clouds offer a unique way to deal with disaster recovery. In a hybrid cloud environment, an enterprise can split workloads between the public and private cloud. For the workloads run in the public cloud, the private cloud could be set up to be the fail-over data center. For the workloads that run in the private cloud, the public cloud could be used as the fail-over data center. To accomplish this, it is important that the public and private cloud leverage the same cloud services as much as possible. Here are a few examples.

Hybrid IaaS Proprietary

Let's assume the proprietary public cloud provider is AWS. In order to keep the systems consistent between the public and private clouds, a private cloud solution that supports AWS APIs must be used. Eucalyptus is one company that supports AWS APIs. It is important to note that Eucalyptus does not support all AWS APIs. Because of this, it makes sense to limit the AWS APIs for the components of the architecture that need to fail over only to those APIs supported by Eucalyptus.

Hybrid IaaS Open

Another option is to leverage an open source IaaS solution like OpenStack and run the software both on the public cloud and the private cloud. In this example, the exact same code can be run on both clouds, and there is no need to limit the use of APIs like there is in the previous Eucalyptus example.

Hybrid PaaS

In order to accomplish fail over between public and private clouds with PaaS, one must first choose a private PaaS. There are several open source and commercial private PaaS players. Many of them are integrated or are in the process of integrating with OpenStack and are capable of running on AWS (or any infrastructure). As mentioned earlier in the book, the downside of private PaaS is that the cloud service consumer still has to manage the infrastructure layer, the application stack, and the PaaS software. But, if fail over is required between public and private clouds, private PaaS is the only solution because public PaaS cannot run on private infrastructure.

AEA CASE STUDY: **Disaster Recovery Planning**

To properly design for disaster recovery, Acme eAuctions (AEA) refers back to its business architecture diagram and assigns a value for the RTO, RPO, and each component of the architecture. The most critical part of the architecture is the buyer services. Every second that buyers can't buy products, AEA is losing revenue. The next most critical component is the API layer. When the API layer is down, external partners cannot access the system. Seller services are the next most critical component. When the seller services are down, new auctions can't be launched and existing auctions can't be changed, but buyers can still bid on active auctions. Of the business processes, the pay seller process can probably be down longer than the other services, but that service is handled by a third-party solution so that AEA does not have to handle credit cards and payments in the cloud. The back-end systems can be down the longest.

The most critical components (buyer services, APIs, seller services) will be architected to run in multiple active-active clouds. AEA has chosen to run in the public cloud. These critical components will be required to run in multiple data centers provided by the cloud service provider. Each data center will run the services as active, and traffic will be routed to the data center closest to the requestor. If that data center is unavailable, the traffic will route to the next available data center. AEA feels that an active-active hot architecture provides it with high availability and fast recovery time. It has also noted plans to leverage its existing data center as another data center to fail over to, but the work required to accomplish that goal is much larger than the time frame AEA currently has to deliver. Instead, the company logs that task in the backlog and ranks it as low for now. If the active-active hot solution in the public cloud does not meet AEA's needs in the future, it can move toward building a hybrid solution so that its data center can also serve as a backup.

The back-end systems follow a more traditional model of backing up data and sending it off-site. A secondary cold site is available to restore services for these components in the event of a disaster.

Summary

Cloud computing is still relatively new and immature. We should expect to see occasional outages, vendors closing their doors, and natural disasters like hurricanes, earthquakes, and floods impacting our ability to keep our systems up all of the time. Planning for disasters is a critical function regardless of the cloud service model. Companies must determine the RTO, RPO, and value of recovery so that the appropriate investments and recovery designs can be implemented. It is critical to understand how to recover from disasters for each cloud service model and each deployment model. The greater the risk of the consequences of a disaster to a company, the more likely the company is going to want more control to mitigate those risks. The risk tolerance can drive the cloud service and deployment model decisions. It is important that disaster recovery is part of the decision-making process when companies choose cloud service and deployment models.

CHAPTER 14

Leveraging a DevOps Culture to Deliver Software Faster and More Reliably

I've hugged a lot of servers in my life. They don't hug you back.
—WERNER VOGEL, CTO OF AMAZON WEB SERVICES

The term *DevOps* is relatively new and broadly misunderstood. Many people think of DevOps as an IT role, more specifically as a hybrid between a developer and a systems administrator. The problem with this thinking is that companies tend to create a new silo called DevOps and try to fill this silo with super-administrators who are magically awesome at both development and operations. Sometimes it is easier to find a unicorn.

DevOps is not a group and it is not a role. DevOps is a culture shift or a new way of thinking about how we develop and release software. The DevOps movement is about tearing down silos and fostering communication and collaboration between development, operations, quality assurance, product, and management.

Developing the DevOps Mind-Set

In 2009, the first DevOps Days conference was held in Belgium where several practitioners, inspired by a presentation by John Allspaw and Paul Hammond titled "10 Deploys per Day: Dev and Ops Cooperation at Flickr," got together to discuss how to create a more collaborative culture among developers and operations. On Twitter, attendees of the conference used the hashtag DevOps to discuss the conference. The topic gained more and more support as more

DevOps Days sprung up across the globe. Eventually, the hashtag became the name of this new movement.

The DevOps movement was born out of frustration of many practitioners' experiences dealing with fragile systems. Systems become fragile due to software being built in silos where the different teams are not communicating effectively with each other. Because of this lack of communication, developers often do not have the environments and tools that they need to be productive, and the operations team often gets software thrown over the wall to them to support. Deployments are complex and error prone, causing release cycles to be longer, thus creating even more risk. These fragile systems are loaded with technical debt, which makes the system harder to maintain with each release.

Fragile systems loaded with technical debt create unplanned work. When resources get pulled off of planned work to jump on unplanned work, project schedules are impacted and due dates slip. In order to mitigate the risks of date slippage, developers are forced to take shortcuts. Shortcuts usually result in a lack of sound architecture, delaying nonfunctional requirements such as security and supportability, and other critical stability features, which leads to even more technical debt. This cycle continues endlessly creating a hopeless death spiral where quality, reliability, morale, and customer satisfaction all degrade over time.

In an effort to stop this madness, the DevOps movement focuses on a systems thinking approach. Early innovators in this space coined the term *CAMS*, which stands for *culture*, *automation*, *measurement*, and *sharing*. The goal of DevOps is not to hire superhuman people who are experts at development and operations; instead, the goal is to build systems with a mind-set that the needs of development, operations, and quality assurance are all interrelated and need to be part of a collaborative process. No longer will developers only be responsible for code, testers only be responsible for testing, and operations only be responsible for operating the system. In a DevOps culture, everyone is responsible and accountable for the entire system. Everyone is on a shared mission with shared incentives. Everyone is responsible for delivery and quality.

DevOps thinking as described by Gene Kim, a notable author and practitioner of DevOps, can be boiled down to these four principles:

1. Understand the flow of work.
2. Always seek to increase flow.
3. Don't pass defects downstream.
4. Achieve a profound understanding of the system.

These principles apply to the entire team. Whether a person is in development, operations, or product, each member of the team should fully understand how the system flows, proactively find ways to improve that flow and eliminate waste, and understand the entire system top to bottom. In addition, the team must insist that defects are not allowed to live on forever because the longer they stick around, the more expensive and complex they are to fix, resulting in unplanned work in the future.

Building and releasing software is a similar process to manufacturing and shipping products. In fact, the DevOps movement is greatly influenced by lean manufacturing principles. One of the main focuses in the DevOps movement is to maximize the flow of software creation from concept to development to release. To accomplish this goal, teams should focus on the following six practices:

1. Automate infrastructure
2. Automate deployments
3. Design for feature flags
4. Measure
5. Monitor
6. Experiment and fail fast

Automate Infrastructure

One of the great advantages of cloud computing is that infrastructure can be abstracted via APIs, thus empowering us with the ability to treat infrastructure as code. Since provisioning and deprovisioning infrastructure can be scripted, there is no excuse not to automate the creation of environments. In fact, we can build code and environments at the same time. A best practice is to enforce the policy that every sprint that ends with a complete set of code should also include the corresponding environment, as well. By enforcing this policy, the user stories in the sprint should include the necessary development, operations, and quality assurance requirements. By delivering the code and its test harnesses with the environment we greatly increase the flow of our work.

In the old days, we would deliver the code, and throw it over the wall to quality assurance, which then threw it over the wall to the operations team that would have to stand up the appropriate environment. Due to a lack of collaboration and communication between these silos, a lot of back-and-forth meetings, phone calls, and e-mails were required in order for operations to attempt to manually create the correct environment. This often led to bottlenecks and environmental issues, since the operations team was not involved in the early discussions. To make matters worse, once the environment was finally completed, the code that was deployed to it was running in this environment for the first time, which usually introduced new bugs late in the project life cycle. Finding bugs late in the life cycle caused teams to prioritize these bugs, only fix the critical ones, and shove the rest into the backlog with tons of other bugs from previous releases that may never make it to the front of the priority list. This is obviously not the way to create quality and speed-to-market.

Operations should empower development to create their own environments, but in a controlled fashion. Providing self-service infrastructure is another great way to increase the flow of development; however, without the right level of governance, self-service can lead to chaos, inconsistent environments, nonoptimized costs, and other bad side-effects. The way to properly allow for self-service provisioning is to create a standard set of machine images that people with the proper access can request on demand. These machine images represent standard machines with all of the proper security controls, policies, and standard software packages installed. For example, a developer may be able to select from a standard set of machine images in a development or quality assurance environment for a web server running Ruby, an application server running NGINX, a database server running MySQL, and so on. The developer does not have to configure any of these environments. Instead he just requests an image and a corresponding target environment. The environment gets automatically provisioned in a few minutes and the developer is off and running. What I just described is how self-service provisioning can work in an Infrastructure as a Service (IaaS) model. In a Platform as a Service (PaaS) model, developers with the appropriate access to nonproduction environments can perform the same self-service functionality using the PaaS user interface.

Automate Deployments

Automating deployments is another critical task for increasing the flow of software development. Many companies have perfected automation deployments to the point where they deploy multiple times a day. To automate deployments, the code, configuration files, and environment scripts should share a single repository. This allows the team to script the deployment process to perform both the build and the corresponding environment at the same time. Automating deployments decreases cycle times because it removes the element of human error from deployments. Faster and better-quality deployments allow teams to deploy more frequently and with confidence. Deploying more frequently leads to smaller change sets, which reduces the risk of failure.

In the old days, deployments were cumbersome manual processes that usually had a dependency on specific people who were knowledgeable about the steps involved to deploy a build. The process was not repeatable because of the manual intervention required and deployments were often dreaded exercises that occurred late at night or early in the morning and involved urgent bug fixing after experiencing issues with the deployment. Since the deployments were challenging and buggy, teams often chose to deploy less frequently due to the fear of breaking the production system.

Automated deployments aim to resolve all of these issues. Automation takes the art out of deployments and makes it easy enough that anyone with the right permissions can deploy software by simply picking a version and an environment and clicking a button. In fact, some companies that have mastered automation require new hires to perform a deployment in a nonproduction environment as part of their training on their first day of work.

Design Feature Flags

Another new trend for modern-day deployment methodologies is the use of feature flags. Feature flags allow features to be configured to be turned on or off or to only be available to a certain group of users. This is useful for a couple of reasons. First, if a feature has issues, once it is deployed it can be quickly configured to be turned off. This allows the rest of the deployed features to remain running in production and gives the team time to fix the issue and redeploy the feature when it is convenient. This approach is much safer than having a team scramble to quickly fix a production issue or cause the entire release to be backed out.

Another use of feature flags is to allow a feature to be tested in production by a select group of users. For example, imagine our fictitious auction company, Acme eAuctions, is launching a new auction feature that allows the person leading a live auction to activate a webcam so the bidding customers can see her. With the feature flag and a corresponding user group setting, this functionality can be turned on for just employees so they can run a mock auction in production and test out the performance and user experience. If the test is acceptable, they may choose to allow the feature to run in a select geography as a beta test to get feedback from customers before rolling it out to all users.

Measure, Monitor, and Experiment

We discussed at length measuring and monitoring in Chapter 12. The point to add here is that by leveraging feature flags, we can run experiments like A/B testing to gather information and learn about the system and its users. For example, let's say that a product manager has a theory that the registration process is too complex for some users and she wants to test a new, simpler registration form. By leveraging feature flags and configurations, the new registration page can be configured to display every other time a registration page is requested so that the team can compare the user metrics of the new registration page against the user metrics of the existing registration page. Another option would be to test the feature in specific geographies, within specific time frames, or for specific browsers or devices.

Feature flags can also be used to test features in production against real production loads. The feature can be enabled for a test group or as a beta launch to a select location. Once enabled, the feature can be closely monitored and turned off once enough data is collected or if any issues are detected. DevOps cultures encourage this type of experimentation. *Fail fast* is a common phrase used in DevOps. With one-click automation of infrastructure and deployments along with the configurability of feature flags, teams can quickly experiment, learn, and adjust, which leads to a better product and happier customers.

Continuous Integration and Continuous Delivery

In our discussion on automation we touched on the automation of environments and builds. Let's dig deeper into this topic. *Continuous integration* (CI) is the practice of building and testing applications on every check-in. No matter how big or small the change is, the developers need to be conditioned to always check in their work.

Continuous delivery (CD) takes this concept one step further and adds automated testing and automated deployment to the process in addition to CI. CD improves the quality of software by ensuring testing is performed throughout the life cycle instead of toward the end. In addition, the build process fails if any automated test fails during the build process. This prevents defects from being introduced into the build, thus improving the overall quality of the system. By leveraging CD, we get software that is always working, and every change that is successfully integrated into a build becomes part of a release candidate.

In the old days, bug fixes that took only a few minutes often had to wait for many other user stories to be completed so they could be packaged up in a big release. In that model, software was assumed to be incorrect until it was validated by dedicated quality assurance professionals. Testing was a phase that was performed after development and the responsibility of quality fell in the hands of the quality assurance team. Developers often threw poor-quality code over the wall to quality assurance in order to meet the development deadlines with little to no repercussions for the quality of their work. Quality assurance often had to cut corners to complete testing to get the code to operations in time to release the software. This resulted in known bugs being allowed to flow into the production system. These bugs would go through a prioritization process where only the most critical bugs would be addressed so that the project data would not be missed or would not slip further.

With CD, software is assumed to be correct unless the automation tells us otherwise. Quality is everyone's responsibility and testing is performed throughout the life cycle. To successfully run projects using continuous delivery, there must be a high level of communication and collaboration along with a sense of trust and ownership throughout the team. In essence, this is the type of culture that the DevOps movement represents.

So, what does all of this stuff have to do with cloud computing? A DevOps culture, continuous integration, and continuous delivery are not mandatory for building software in the cloud. In fact, to large, established companies with tons of process and long delivery cycles this may all sound more like a fantasy than reality. But all three of these buzzwords evolved from innovative practitioners leveraging one of the biggest advantages of cloud computing, infrastructure as code, and putting it to use with some tried-and-tested best practices from lean manufacturing.

One of the biggest promises of cloud computing is agility. Each cloud service model provides us with an opportunity to get to market faster than ever before. But it takes more than the technology to realize that agility. As every enterprise architect knows, it takes people, process, and technology. The technology is here now. People like you are reading books like this because you want to learn how to take advantage of this amazing technology to achieve business goals. But without good process, agility will be hard to come by. Here is a real-life example.

A client of mine built an amazing cloud architecture that changed the business landscape in its industry. This client turned the business model upside down within its industry, because all of its competitors had legacy systems in massive data centers and large investments of infrastructure spread throughout retail customer stores. This client built an entire solution in a public cloud and required no infrastructure at the retail stores, resulting in quicker implementations, drastically lower costs, and more flexibility. Unfortunately, as my client grew from a small start-up to a large company it did not establish a mature set of processes for builds and deployments. It created a silo of operations personnel, dubbed "DevOps." Developers threw code over the wall to quality assurance, which threw it over the wall to DevOps. DevOps became a huge bottleneck. The goal of this team was to automate the builds and the deployments. The problem was that it was not a shared responsibility. Everything fell into this group's lap and it could only chip away at the problem. The end result was a lot of missed deadlines, poor success rates of deployments, poor quality, angry customers, and low morale. Even though the company's technology was superior to the competition, the bottlenecks within IT were so great that it could not capitalize by quickly adding more features to differentiate itself from the market even more.

The moral of the story is cloud technologies by themselves are not enough. It takes great people, a special culture of teamwork and ownership, and great processes, which should include as much automation as possible in order to achieve agility in the cloud.

Summary

DevOps is a grassroots cultural movement driven mostly by operations practitioners, with the goal of increasing collaboration and communication among team members to release quality software quicker and more reliably. DevOps should not be thought of as an IT role and should not be another silo within IT. The DevOps mind-set is based on lean manufacturing principles with the goals of increasing work flow and eliminating waste while reducing defects.

Continuous integration is a common process used in DevOps cultures, which practices building and testing the system with every check-in. Continuous delivery strives to increase the rate at which software can be deployed by enforcing automated tests, builds, and deployments. Companies looking to the cloud for agility must not forget that it takes the right culture (people) and processes like CI and CD along with the technology to accomplish the goal of delivering on agility.

References

Duvall, P., S. Matyas, and A. Glover (2007). *Continuous Integration: Improving Software Quality and Reducing Risk*. Upper Saddle River, NJ: Addison-Wesley.

Humble, J., and D. Farley (2010). *Continuous Delivery: Reliable Software Releases Through Build, Test, and Deployment Automation*. Upper Saddle River, NJ: Addison-Wesley.

Kim, G. (2012, September 27). "Why We Need DevOps." Puppet Conference 2012. Keynote address. Mission Bay Conference Center, San Francisco.

CHAPTER 15

Assessing the Organizational Impact of the Cloud Model

People don't hate change, they hate the way you're trying to change them.

—MICHAEL T. KANAZAWA, TRANSFORMATION CHANGE EXPERT

If we look back at the evolution of technology from the mainframe days, to the birth of the personal computer to the Internet age, and now the cloud, the one thing that is constant about these transitions is that they all bring a tremendous amount of change. Along with the change in technology, come changes in how businesses operate. Each transition altered the operating model of businesses. In the mainframe days, software was primarily used to support internal business functions like payroll, accounting, manufacturing, and the like. Consumers did not interface with systems, they interfaced with people like bank tellers, cashiers, insurance agents, pharmacists, travel agents, and so forth. Business and IT alignment was much easier back then because IT's sole purpose was to build applications for the business.

The PC era created a new operating model where software vendors would package and ship software to customers, who would install and manage the software within their own enterprises. This new operating model required organizational changes in order for companies to support software that was running at customer sites. New support organizations were formed, new sales processes were created, and new software requirements were prioritized to deal with software running at client sites. Pricing models changed, incentives changed, contracts and terms of services changed, and even the types of customers changed. Business and IT alignment started to fragment because now IT had many customers, internal and external. In addition, IT now had to manage infrastructure and software distributed within and outside the enterprise, whereas in the past everything was centralized on the mainframe.

The Internet era changed the operating model drastically again by allowing businesses to sell goods and services directly to customers 24 hours a day. Now businesses could operate around the clock and outside of brick-and-mortar buildings. As in the previous era, huge process and strategy changes impacted sales, legal, development, support, and so forth. IT now had not only to deal with internal and external customers; consumers now were directly talking to systems. On top of that, internal systems were now at risk of being compromised by all kinds of external threats that could enter via the Internet. This created a huge gap in IT and business alignment because even more non-value-added work was thrust upon IT departments.

Now the cloud is here and the pattern of change is repeating itself once again. Cloud computing brings an enormous amount of change to a businesses operating model. These changes go way beyond the IT department and companies need to be prepared to tackle them. Now IT is building software that runs in the cloud and customers access it via the Internet. The days of shipping software to a customer and making a killing in professional services and annual maintenance fees are over. Large licensing fees and large capital expenditures coupled with long implementation projects are a distant memory. The expectation now is that the software is turned on, always works, gets updated regularly, and we only pay for what we use. Talk about change! Let's take a closer look at how these changes impact organizations.

Enterprise Model vs. Elastic Cloud Model

Prior to the rise in cloud computing, many companies participated in what is called the *on-premises software delivery model*, also known as the *enterprise model*. In this model, companies built and managed their own data centers and infrastructure and built software that was either shipped to customers or downloaded by customers. In the software delivery model, major releases of software were typically delivered annually or semiannually with small patches during the year to fix critical defects or release an important feature.

The software was built with the intention that the customer or a professional services company would perform an install or an upgrade of an existing install. Upgrades were disruptive to the customers' day-to-day business. Customers had plenty of other priorities and did not want to be updating vendor solutions too frequently. The customer also was responsible for managing the physical infrastructure and the software, which included capacity planning, backup/recovery, and scaling. When systems were nearing capacity, the customer was responsible for procuring more hardware and more licenses. Purchasing this type of software required up-front capital for hardware, software, and human resources needed to implement the solutions. Many software products required long, complex implementations that might take weeks or even months. Other solutions required specialists to be brought in at outrageous hourly rates to perform the install of these proprietary solutions. Companies' revenue models banked on professional services and reoccurring annual maintenance fees that averaged 20 percent of the initial cost. In this model, changes to the software happened infrequently, because of the complexity and the costs of performing upgrades.

Enter the cloud era and the new operating model, called the *elastic cloud model*. Randy Bias, chief technology officer of Cloudscaling, said it best in an interview that I did with him: "There is a fundamental shift in software that ships versus software that is hosted." The shift caused by the elastic cloud model is as disruptive to businesses as the impacts of the Internet were back in the 1990s. In the enterprise model, once the vendors created and shipped a release, the onus was on the customer to manage the production environment. In the elastic model, the cloud providers are delivering a service that is always on, like a utility. Building cloud services raises the level of quality, speed-to-market, and customer focus that an organization must provide to stay competitive.

Here is an analogy that sums up the difference between the enterprise model and the elastic model. The enterprise model is like selling a generator to a customer and the elastic model is the equivalent of providing the electricity to a customer 24 hours a day. Once you build and ship the generator you are done with the customer interaction except for customer support calls. When providing electricity, the job is never done because the electricity must always work. If the generator breaks, only one customer is unhappy. If the electricity does not work, a lot of customers are unhappy. Obviously, the company providing electricity requires a very different organization than the company selling generators.

IT Impact

The following sections highlight the areas within IT that are impacted when moving from an on-premises enterprise model to an elastic cloud model.

- **Deployments.** Deployments in the cloud happen frequently and in flight without downtime as opposed to shipping patches or full releases and relying on customers or field service technicians to install the software.
- **Customer support.** The cloud vendor will be responsible for all infrastructure, autoscaling, patching/upgrading, security vulnerabilities, service level agreements (SLAs), and more. Customer support will

expand beyond application support and will now extend to 24-by-7-by-365 real-time support of a highly reliable, scalable, and auditable platform.

- **Regulatory**. Cloud-based software is held to a much higher standard than shipped software. Because customers are giving up control of the infrastructure, data, security, and the SLA, they shift a lot of responsibility to the cloud vendor. Along with that responsibility come regulatory requirements such as SAS70, SSAE 16, HIPAA, SOX, PCI, and more. Customers that are bound by these regulations will require that their providers are compliant, as well.

- **Monitoring**. Running a real-time platform requires rigorous monitoring, logging, and system-level metrics collecting. The best platforms take a very proactive approach and look for variances in their data to head off problems before they become catastrophic. For example, if a certain API is called 1,000 times a day on average but all of a sudden it is called 5 times or 5,000 times, somebody should look at the logs and see if something is starting to go wrong. Organizations must be more proactive in their monitoring in the elastic model.

- **Availability**. With shipped software it is up to the customer to manage the infrastructure and perform the appropriate capacity planning. With hosted software the vendor must meet or beat published SLAs. To do this the vendor must deliver extremely high-quality software that can be updated seamlessly without downtime. In addition, the software must automatically scale up and down to handle traffic peaks and be able to fail over automatically in the event of a data center failure.

- **Independence**. With shipped software, customer independence is easy. Each customer gets software shipped to it and each customer is mutually exclusive from any other customer. In a multitenant environment this is much harder to achieve. Most cloud vendors will want to use shared resources as much as possible to keep costs down, but they may also need to segregate certain components like data, billing information, and performance so that clients can't access competitor information and to prevent a performance hit in one client from impacting the others.

Business Impacts

Cloud computing's impacts go far beyond the walls of IT. It is critical that the business impacts are understood, as well. The following sections will discuss the impacts to the accounting and finance, legal, sales, and human resources departments.

Accounting and Finance

Cash flow is one of the most important pieces of financial information that investors and shareholders look for in financial statements. Cash flow is simply the difference between how much money flows into the company (revenues) and the amount of money that flows out (expenses). Cloud computing changes both the sources of revenue and the outgoing cash. In the enterprise operating model, packaged software was purchased up front before the software was installed and put to use. There was usually an annual maintenance fee that ranged from 18 to 20 percent of the initial purchase price. Sometimes there was also a professional services charge for the installation of the software, which might be a multiweek or multimonth effort. From the seller's perspective, sales were fairly predictable because the pricing was a known entity and easy to forecast. For buyers, a large up-front investment was required, which negatively impacted cash flow. It would take time for the revenues generated (if this even was a revenue-generating tool) to cover the up-front capital expenditure.

In the elastic operating model, the cash flow story is much different. Most cloud services are sold as a pay-as-you-go model where buyers have no up-front costs and only pay for the amount of services they use. Some cloud services charge a monthly subscription fee, but there is still no large investment to get started. As a buyer, the capital expenditure (CAPEX) is removed from the equation, and the cost of the service is categorized as an operating expense (OPEX). The buyer pays for the cloud service at a rate that is proportional to the rate at which it brings in revenue or value to the organization. For example, a company leveraging Infrastructure as a Service (IaaS) pays for the amount of compute capacity required to launch its first customer. As the company starts to acquire more customers, it ramps up its spending with its IaaS provider in support of the increased incoming revenues. If managed properly, the company scales its costs with its revenues, and the costs are considered OPEX. This approach frees up working capital to invest in other areas of the business.

One challenge that the pay-as-you-go model presents is that the predictability of revenues and costs is much more dynamic than in the enterprise model. In the enterprise model, a customer paid an initial cost, which was a one-time fixed cost. Annual maintenance costs were very predictable. If the customer needed to buy more, it went through a procurement process, which was easily tracked. In the elastic model, the seller has very little control over the amount the customer spends because the customer is consuming services on-demand as needed. One month a customer may use 25 percent more services than the next. Forecasting becomes much less predictable as both the revenues and the operating expenses fluctuate based on usage.

The product team should work closely with the finance team to determine the optimal pricing structure that satisfies the needs of both customer acquisition and corporate finance and accounting.

Legal

Contracts for cloud-based software and services are much more advanced than contracts for shipped software. These new contracts have specific language around privacy, data ownership, and numerous other regulations such as SSAE 16, HIPAA, PCI, and more. The due diligence process for both the buyer and seller of cloud-based software and services is much more robust and time consuming than in traditional enterprise software because the vendor is taking on more responsibilities on behalf of the customer. Also, the laws and regulations are changing as regulators are being pushed to update their policies to accommodate the digital era. In my experience, buyers of cloud services are much more demanding and more rigorous in the vetting process, especially around privacy, security, SLAs, and certifications. The amount of time it takes to close a deal for a cloud-based B2B service far exceeds what it took when I was making noncloud-based software sales to enterprises.

The legal department should prepare for more requests and more thorough evaluations of products and services. If this group is not prepared for the increase in work, it could become a bottleneck and slow down customer acquisition. In extreme cases where the competition is fierce, a bottleneck in legal could cause the deal to be lost. A best practice is to produce a document that spells out all of the policies and procedures pertaining to privacy, security, regulations, SLAs, ownership, and so forth. Some companies create two documents. The first is a high-level public document that does not require a nondisclosure agreement to be signed and that can be handed out to potential customers and even posted on the company website. A second document is a more detailed standard document that sums up all of the legal information that would be in a contract. The quicker the seller can put the customer at ease, the faster it can close the deal. Without these documents there is a risk of endless requests for information from customers.

Sales

Selling cloud-based software and services requires that salespeople upgrade their technical skills. Salespeople must, at a minimum, understand the basics of cloud computing and be able to discuss things like privacy and SLAs at a high level. For the next few years until cloud computing becomes the norm for companies, salespeople will have to spend as much time selling the value of cloud computing as they will selling the value of their product.

Selling in the elastic model is very different from selling the enterprise model. Obviously the pay-as-you-go pricing model is very different from the large up-front acquisition model. In many cases, buyers are not locked into long-term commitments and simply pay by the month. The time it takes to implement a solution is drastically reduced as well, in most cases. In the past, there was usually a long procurement process that included hardware, software, professional services, and project plan for implementation. In the elastic model, many services can be turned on instantly as soon as the buyer agrees to the terms. Often the entire sales process occurs with no intervention from the seller. Buyers can go to the sellers' websites and click a few buttons and start consuming services. In such cases, the selling process is more focused on advertising and raising awareness through social media, conferences, e-mail campaigns, and many other media outlets.

Just because cloud software can be turned on with the click of a button and the registration of a credit card, does not mean that enterprises will forgo the evaluation process. It really depends on the service that is being provided. An IT team looking for a collaboration tool may make that decision without a robust evaluation and sign up quickly to start using the tool. A company trying to decide between IaaS vendors may perform a very thorough evaluation, including several meetings with each provider with detailed discussions concerning finance and legal.

Human Resources

Many companies do not have the required skill sets for cloud computing, so human resources (HR) will be asked to find cloud-ready employees. Not every city has a surplus of cloud talent, which will require recruiters to look both nationally and globally. Many cloud experts will not want to relocate, so remote employment will be a key to acquiring talent. HR will have to balance leveraging full-time employees with consultants to get the right mix of talent required to take on the challenges of cloud computing. There are a large number of cloud consulting companies, but buyer beware. Just about any company that was in the consulting business is now magically a cloud consulting company. There is a good chance that anyone who reads this book front to back knows way more about cloud computing than the high-priced consultants that claim to have expertise. Interview these consulting firms as if they were applying for full-time positions within your company. Don't be fooled by the marketing slides and fancy business cards. Cloud computing is very new to enterprises and very few people or companies have relevant experience yet.

For companies building cloud solutions, it is highly recommended that they evaluate existing rewards and recognition programs to see if they make sense for today's software development methods. In Chapter 14, we discussed how important it is to break down the silos in IT. Throughout this book it has been stressed how critical it is to build loosely coupled services. HR and IT should brainstorm ways to foster this desired behavior. If the current incentives do not encourage people to make this change, then it is foolish to think that things will magically change. Evaluate the existing organizational structure and make sure it is optimized for information sharing, learning, and silo busting. Create a DevOps culture that prides itself on teamwork and collaboration. Reward people for the new behavior and discourage the old behavior.

Organization Change Planning

In order to succeed as an organization, our fictitious company, AEA, needs a change management plan to lead it through this transformation. The CRM project is just the tip of the iceberg for change. There is substantial change required to deliver the future version of the auction site that will be a Platform as a Service (PaaS) solution connecting third parties to the auction engine.

The consequences of organizational resistance to change are poor implementations, projects that take too long and cost too much, and projects that don't deliver expected results. In the most extreme cases, the company does not embrace the change and reverts back to its old ways. To combat these undesirable results, change expert John Kotter recommends an eight-step process to lead transformational change through the organization:

1. Establish a sense of urgency.
2. Create a guiding coalition.
3. Develop a vision and strategy
4. Communicate the change vision.
5. Empower people to drive the vision.
6. Create short-term wins.
7. Consolidate gains and produce more change.
8. Anchor new approaches in the culture.

Let's see how Acme eAuctions (AEA) used Kotter's eight steps to deal with the resistance from within the organization.

AEA CASE STUDY: Organization Change Planning

In Chapter 3, we discussed the internal resistance of the AEA SaaS CRM project. The development team that wrote the legacy CRM system was resisting the decision to replace it with a new, modern SaaS solution.

After several months of not making any progress on implementing the new SaaS-based CRM application, AEA's CIO, Shirley Davidson, hired Fred Sanders, a long-time expert on organizational change management.

Fred worked with Shirley to start a communication strategy for AEA. The first step was to create a sense of urgency. They drafted a message that talked about how the new system would empower the sales force with mobile and social capabilities, thus allowing the team to be more responsive and customer friendly. The message also talked about the financial benefits to the company, including reduced costs, opportunity costs of redeploying internal resources to high-priority initiatives, and less hardware and software to maintain, patch, and upgrade. The third part of the message discussed the real-time and analytical capabilities that would give the sales team a competitive advantage by producing better lead generation, more collaboration, and more personalization for customers. The final piece of the message was to tie the delivery of this initiative to the critical path for sales hitting their stretch goals for the year-end. This would help the company reach its target numbers, thus giving all employees a chance to receive their full bonus at the end of the year.

Shirley and Fred then assembled a team (the guiding coalition) that was responsible for the delivery of both the project and the transformation. The team was made up of people across the organization who were both influential and respected. The team had a representative from finance, one from human resources, a middle manager from the infrastructure team, a director from application development, and an architect. Each one of these people had a center of influence within his or her area of expertise and could explain the question "What's in it for me?" (WIIFM) for each employee. At the heart of all change is answering WIIFM for each person affected. Once people know why they are being asked to change, what that change means to them and the organization, and why it is urgent, the odds of their supporting the change increase dramatically.

Once the team was formed, it was tasked with taking the urgency statement and creating a vision to be communicated throughout the organization. The vision clearly articulated the future state and the improvements to the overall effectiveness of sales due to these changes. Once the vision was formed, the team created a communication plan that included a town hall meeting to discuss the urgency and the vision and answer any questions. Each member held small team meetings with various teams throughout the organization to discuss the change in terms that were relevant to each team. For example, the finance team meeting focused on the changes involved from buying software licenses and hardware up-front to paying for services on demand. The application development team's discussion focused on moving away from building noncore-competency applications in favor of integrating SaaS solutions. Each team meeting zeroed in on what was most important for that group. Different members of the guiding coalition blogged about the project and wrote articles in the monthly newsletter. They communicated the vision often and through multiple channels.

The team was empowered to make decisions, including removing any obstacles in the way, whether those obstacles were created by conflicting priorities or by resistance. Any blockers that they could not resolve would be referred to Shirley. In one instance, Shirley had to let go of an employee because of the negative influence that the person was creating. Once the communication plan kicked in, the project took off again, and in one month the program to migrate the data from the old system to the new SaaS-based system was developed and tested. The cutover was scheduled for early one Saturday morning. The data was imported into the system. The users and testers accessed the data all weekend and the team cut over on Monday morning. The feedback from sales was tremendous, and the team was rewarded with a catered lunch and gift cards to share with their families.

The next step was to use this project as a case study to promote more change within the company. The people on the team could now be evangelists for more SaaS-based solutions going forward. Fred's job here was done. He and Shirley had created change and institutionalized that change as the new way to do business. Without the investment in organizational change management, AEA would likely not have completed the migration to SaaS and would be continuing to pay for a legacy system that was not meeting anybody's needs.

Change in the Real World

I realize that the AEA change management example may sound more like a fairy tale than a real-world solution. Many years ago, I led a large service-oriented architecture initiative that required drastic change throughout the organization. Not only did it require IT to work across silos, it also required the business to drastically change business processes. There was a tremendous amount of resistance that was interfering with progress. At the time, I was earning my MBA at night when I discovered Kotter's work in one of my classes. His ideas hit home and I bought and read more of his books on change. Feeling optimistic and energized, I returned to work and started implementing Kotter's eight steps. It was challenging because we were already far down the road and resistance had already been established. But we made progress, especially where we could get the middle managers engaged. Some folks were just never going to get on board and it wasn't easy, but had we not started implementing organizational change management plans, the project might have failed. The lesson learned is to implement this plan early and create a positive vibe before resistance settles in.

Summary

Moving from an enterprise model to an elastic compute model is an organization-wide effort that should not be underestimated. Not only is it a shift in technology strategy, but it is also a shift in strategy across all departments. Management should analyze each department within the company and identify the changes required to move the organization into an elastic cloud-operating model. Companies that recognize this and make the appropriate changes throughout the organization will have a higher degree of success than those companies that see it only as an IT project.

References

Kotter, John P. (1996). *Leading Change*. Boston: Harvard Business School Press.

Kotter, John P., and Dan S. Cohen (2002). *The Heart of Change: Real-Life Stories of How People Change Their Organizations*. Boston: Harvard Business School Press.

The Open Group (2013). "Building Return on Investment from Cloud Computing: Discussion: Financial Value Perspective of Moving from CAPEX to OPEX and Pay-as-You-Go." Retrieved from http://www.opengroup.org/cloud/whitepapers/ccroi/disc1.htm.

Ross, S. A., R. W. Westerfield, and B. D. Jordan (2012). *Fundamentals of Corporate Finance*. Boston: McGraw-Hill Irwin.

CHAPTER 16

Final Thoughts

People in any organization are always attracted to the obsolete—the things that should have worked but did not, the things that once were productive and no longer are.

—PETER DRUCKER

C loud computing will disrupt today's businesses in countless ways. Start-ups have been blazing the trail by embracing the pay-as-you-go model and quickly bringing innovative solutions to market at a fraction of the price that was possible in the past. At the time this book was being written, enterprises were reaching a tipping point where they were finally overcoming their fears of the cloud and were starting to make substantial investments to start moving workloads into the cloud. Cloud computing is relatively imma-ture, but it is evolving rapidly. So much has changed in the time while I was writing this book that I had to go back and update many chapters after I com-pleted the first version. The speed at which change is happening is remark-able. We have entered a golden era of innovation, and I truly believe that the cloud era long term will have as big of an impact on society as the industrial age did, if not bigger.

The Cloud Is Evolving Rapidly

When I first started building software in the cloud back in 2008, Infrastructure as a Service (IaaS) was only being used by start-ups and websites or for ad hoc tasks, but hardly any enterprises were using it for anything substantial. Enter-prises were concerned about the lack of security and reliability in the public cloud. The early adopters of the public cloud were launching innovative busi-nesses at record speeds and with very little capital. As success stories started piling up over the next few years enterprises kept evaluating but the cloud solu-tions were not yet up to corporate standards. Then the private cloud started becoming very appealing to enterprises. They could now build their own clouds and take on the responsibility of security, regulations, and availability.

As enterprises started down the private cloud path they started to realize that it was a lot more work than they expected and could be a complex undertaking, because of all of the existing legacy applications that were not architected to run in the cloud. They also realized that they were not getting all of the benefits of cloud computing, such as rapid elasticity and ubiquitous network access. As enterprises pushed forward they started looking at hybrid clouds, which is where many Fortune 1000 companies' mind-sets were at the time this book was being written.

The large enterprises are driving the innovation within the cloud vendor community because the vendors know that the best path to revenue is through the budgets of the big enterprises. Private Platform as a Service (PaaS) has emerged as a hot item, whereas two years ago it was not even on the radar; after all, the purpose of PaaS was to not have to manage any infrastructure or application stacks. What the vendors soon learned is that as appealing as it sounds to not have to manage any infrastructure, it is not an important requirement for large enterprises. Most large enterprises want the agility and "infrastructure as code" capabilities of the cloud, but they still want to control their own destiny in certain areas when it comes to storing data and managing service level agreements (SLAs). What is becoming a common practice today is large enterprises building hybrid cloud architectures and then evaluating workloads on a case-by-case basis to determine which workloads they can put in the public cloud and which ones go in their private cloud.

Another area that has evolved rapidly is the rise of cloud services that focus on a specific process or technological hurdle. For example, there are Software as a Service (SaaS) and PaaS solutions for almost every function within today's architectures. Here are some examples of services that solve a particular IT problem.

- Security services
- Performance testing
- Continuous integration and delivery platforms (a.k.a. DevOps)
- Web vulnerability scanning
- Database services
- Caching services
- Logging services
- Monitoring services
- Intrusion detection
- Mobile development platforms
- Big-data platforms
- Social media platforms

The list goes on and on. Almost any function that IT has to address in today's architectures is available as a service. What that means is that building solutions in the cloud today can be radically accelerated by integrating a collection of cloud services as opposed to building everything from scratch. By leveraging these cloud services, companies can focus more on their core competencies and get their products and services to market faster.

Another area that is evolving rapidly is the processes and methodologies that companies are embracing to build cloud services. We discussed the lean-thinking mentality of the DevOps culture in Chapter 14. Companies are taking advantage of the speed-to-market gains from being able to provision infrastructure in minutes and are treating infrastructure just like software. The speed at which infrastructure can be provisioned has caused IT shops to rethink their old methodologies. Many companies are starting to emulate the success stories of companies like Etsy, LinkedIn, Amazon, HubSpot, and others that deploy many times a day. Vendors are quickly bringing tools to the marketplace to assist in continuous integration, delivery, and deployments. We are seeing agility like never before in the history of computing. As more companies start embracing the DevOps model, more CIOs are going to demand similar results from their teams. It is going to be interesting to see how this plays out over the next several years. My assumption is that the IT shops that do not embrace this mentality will be at risk of having their departments outsourced once deploying daily becomes the new normal. This leads to the next section called "Cloud Culture."

Cloud Culture

Those of us who grew up before the 1990s, often joke about how the younger generation does not know what an 8-track player is, what a rotary phone looks like, what cars without automatic windows and locks are like, or what life was like without smartphones. Obviously, the younger generation sees the world differently than the generations that came before them. The same holds true for companies. There are many companies that were born in the cloud era. These companies don't worry about a lot of the things that legacy companies worry about. All they know is cloud. All they have ever practiced is agile. They work from anywhere and anytime of the day and only need connectivity and a browser to get work done. Things that require drastic change for legacy companies come naturally to these cloud cultures. This generation grew up with mobile devices, social networks, freemium business models, open source software, and self-service.

The cloud culture only knows a world that is cloudy. Since this generation has never had to deal with mainframes, large enterprise systems like

SAP, locked-down corporate desktops, seven layers of management, and all the glory of working in large enterprises, they are able to think and innovate with fewer constraints than those who came before them. The result is that this generation and these new cloud-only companies are where much of today's innovation is coming from. Large companies are taking notice and what we are seeing is mergers and acquisitions becoming a key strategy for large companies to acquire cloud computing talent. Another reason why there are so many mergers and acquisitions today is that business models are changing and the old enterprise models are falling out of favor. Large companies that survive on hardware and software sales are finding out that their business models are outdated in this new era. Mergers and acquisitions are a quick way to get back in the game.

New Business Models

Today's start-ups are able to take a hypothesis and test it in the marketplace quickly without a huge up-front investment by leveraging a combination of IaaS, PaaS, and SaaS solutions. We have seen a few consumer-facing website companies like Instagram and Tumblr go from a small start-up to a billion-dollar company in just a few years. Companies like these are outliers. It is rare that a company has the success that these two web gems have had. What is emerging is a different kind of business model, the pay-as-you-go business-to-business model. Start-ups no longer need to invent some incredibly unique idea to launch a business anymore. What we are seeing in the marketplace today is a lot of legacy software that is expensive, cumbersome to use, and outdated. This creates great opportunities for new companies to update the technology.

Much of today's enterprise software is sold by large, billion-dollar companies that have acquired solutions from smaller companies and integrated them into one big software package. The software is expensive and complex to install, maintain, and use. There are licensing fees, upgrades, training expenses, and other costs. To make matters worse, much of the software we use today in our personal life is simple, works on mobile devices and tablets, is integrated with social, and requires no training. What I see emerging is that start-ups are not inventing new things; they are taking a business process that is being poorly serviced by today's legacy software or is not being serviced at all, and providing that business process as a service using new technology.

The health-care industry is loaded with start-ups that are automating archaic manual processes such as processing claims, tracking equipment in hospitals, and reducing service times. Workday is a SaaS solution for human resource management. It is rapidly grabbing market share in large enterprises. There is nothing new about the concept of human resource management. What is new is the way Workday delivers the service. This SaaS solution requires no hardware, no maintenance, no resources to manage it, no licensing fees, and no annual upgrades. But it is more than just delivering it as SaaS that is the difference maker. By building this solution from scratch, Workday was able to architect a highly scalable solution that supports modern devices and tablets, leverages big-data analytics, and has prebuilt connectors for integration with other enterprise applications. Companies that embrace cloud computing have a unique opportunity to take market share away from traditional software companies by serving customers better with more modern applications in a pay-as-you-go model.

The big companies are not just going to sit there and lose market share, however. They are buying these companies as they start to gain traction in the marketplace. Just like in the past, the big vendors will buy up these competitors and integrate them into a one-size-fits-all enterprise offering. The difference this time is that these new cloud-based applications are built for integration. In the past, it was cumbersome integrating different technology stacks with closed architectures. Today's cloud architectures are based on RESTful (Representational State Transfer) services and were designed to be loosely coupled. My prediction is that the big vendors will initially lose some market share but will eventually buy up the top-tier SaaS and PaaS solutions and offer an impressive collection of pay-as-you-go services that customers can configure to their liking. The cloud era presents a huge opportunity for start-ups to enter the marketplace and for large companies to acquire innovation. It is going to be quite a ride the next few years.

PaaS Is the Game Changer

The one area that I think will have the biggest impact of them all is PaaS. Often when people think of PaaS they think about a development platform for .NET or LAMP stack developers, but that is just the tip of the iceberg. Other PaaS solutions that will make a huge impact are the ones that focus on mobile and big data. Building mobile applications is a challenging task. There are so many different smartphones and feature phones as well as tablets, which require customizations in order for the user interface to render correctly. Companies often pay for developers to build one version for iOS, another for Android, another for iPad, and so on. Mobile PaaS companies are emerging that allow the designers and developers to build one version and deploy to the devices of choice. The PaaS takes care of dealing with the complexities of multiple devices. These PaaS solutions create enormous speed-to-market capabilities and allow developers to spend their development time focusing on new features instead of focusing on the underlying technology, which is constantly changing.

With big data, we are now able to process enormous amounts of data and produce actionable results faster than ever before. Advances in this area are producing better knowledge about customers, and real-time information about Internet-connected devices like the health of a car or an airplane engine, and making it easier to discover patterns in data like never before. The challenge is that it is fairly complicated to set up and manage the databases and infrastructure required to tackle big-data problems. Big-data PaaS solutions are emerging that take the rocket science out of setting up and managing these complex environments. As these PaaS solutions start to mature, any company will be able to implement a big-data solution by leveraging a pay-as-you-go cloud service as opposed to investing a lot of time, money, and resources trying to figure it out by themselves.

It is these PaaS solutions that automate specific, complex problems that will make a huge difference in time-to-market in the future. Companies will be able to leverage multiple PaaS solutions to quickly build new products and services with limited staff and limited budgets. PaaS is still early in the maturity phase and is not widely adopted yet. In a few more years, as it matures and more companies start to embrace it, we will see new products and services come to market quicker than ever before. Mark my words: PaaS will have the biggest impact on productivity since the transition from punchcards to Windows-based systems.

AEA CASE STUDY: **Final Architecture**

Acme eAuctions (AEA) has completed its preliminary design discussions in sprint 0. It has also completed a considerable amount of research through reading books and blogs, attending conferences, going to meetups, and watching webinars. Out of the three key variables—time, money, and resources—time is the most fixed at six months. Since time is short, AEA has decided to leverage PaaS and SaaS as much as possible. This decision shifts more responsibility to the cloud service providers, thus freeing up IT to focus more on core competencies.

Starting at the top of the business architecture diagram, AEA has chosen to evaluate API management SaaS solutions. These solutions will allow AEA to connect the API layer to external partners much quicker, because the SaaS tools will handle integrating with the various technology stacks and communication protocols. These solutions will also provide logging, monitoring, security, and analytics for all APIs.

AEA also decided to leverage a Mobile Backend as a Service (mBaaS) solution to speed up the delivery of the user interface across multiple devices. The developers will be able to get to market much faster because they only need to create a single user interface, and the mBaaS solution will take care of transforming their design to the many devices in the marketplace.

AEA also selected a PaaS solution to expedite the following workflow processes: create content, list content, fulfill order, process payment, and pay seller. It chose to build the auction product process on IaaS because of the extreme processing requirements. The auctions are transactional processes that must meet high-performance requirements and have the ability to scale up and down on demand, and require the most control. Another determining factor is that the legacy system has an auction engine that works in the on-premises environment. It does not have the elasticity that the future state architecture requires, but it does work well under current loads. The team felt that to meet the six-month deliverable to connect partners to the platform, it would hold the auction engine rewrite out of scope for now. Instead the developers will implement a hybrid cloud solution that leverages a public PaaS to drive most of the workflow but leverage the existing auction engine in the existing data center.

The back-end systems are all roadmap items for future SaaS replacements, given that none of them are a core competency. The only exception is the CRM migration to SaaS, which was already completed.

The AEA infrastructure team selected a logging and monitoring tool that is both supported by the public PaaS and can be run in a data center or on any PaaS. This approach allows for centralizing logging and monitoring functionality. All personally identifiable information (PII) is designed to reside in an encrypted database table hanging off the customer table. All data travels over HTTPS and the PII data is also stored encrypted. No other data is stored encrypted so that the performance won't be impacted.

Many of the buyer and seller services leveraged third-party services. For example, AEA chose not to write its own My Cart and Payments modules in the buyer services or the Advertise module in the seller services.

The disaster recovery plan for the PaaS solution is to get regular backups of data from the cloud database. The recovery time objective (RTO) and the recovery point objective (RPO) for the services deployed in the PaaS are higher than the RTO and RPO of the auction engine. Since the auction engine is still on-premises, the existing disaster recovery plan for it still applies. Down the road, when AEA rewrites the auction engine, it will build an active-active hot solution to maximize uptime.

AEA was able to lay out its plan and a roadmap for the remaining components because it took some time up front and applied a pragmatic approach. Now that it has a clear direction and strategy it can start sprinting. Had the company started sprinting right away, it would have been difficult to put a cohesive strategy together and it would have risked making the wrong cloud service model and deployment model decisions, which it would pay for dearly for years to come.

Summary

Cloud computing has reached a tipping point where it has passed the hype phase and has entered a phase where enterprises are starting to embrace the fact that the cloud is real and here to stay. Like any other new idea or technology, there are no silver bullets. The companies that will have success in the cloud are the ones that understand the differences between the cloud service and deployment models and make the right choices based on the business requirements of their company. They must understand the technical requirements for building cloud services and implement an architecture that addresses each requirement. These companies must also deal with organizational change and manage against resistance, skill-set gaps, new processes, and more. As with any other transformation that we have dealt with over the years, it all comes down to people, process, and the technology.

In today's environment, companies can quickly leverage a combination of many different cloud services to get new innovative products to market faster and cheaper than ever before. Now that enterprises and governments are investing heavily in cloud technologies, hybrid models are becoming more mature. With the increase of trust in hybrid models, cloud adoption is quickly rising and the barriers to entry are lowering. Procuring and managing infrastructure is becoming less of a bottleneck now that provisioning infrastructure can be done through code. And given that infrastructure can be treated as code, practitioners are looking at new ways of building and managing software to increase agility. The DevOps movement is an important cultural shift that has emerged. Companies that have embraced and perfected lean thinking are able to build highly reliable systems that can react to business needs much faster than ever before. Some companies actually deploy multiple times a day.

All of this is leading to new business models and the opportunity for any company to embrace emerging technologies like mobile, big data, social media marketing, and others without being required to be experts at the underlying technologies. The rate of change is accelerating faster than ever before and we are on the verge of an unprecedented technology revolution. The companies that embrace cloud computing and are pragmatic about their approach to building cloud services will be a big part of this change. The companies that resist cloud computing or rush to build solutions without an understanding of what is required to properly architect cloud services will likely not be around when the dust settles from all of this change.

Companies should accept the fact that cloud computing is here to stay. When building solutions in the cloud expect constant change. We are still early in this evolving space. Today, hybrid clouds are popular. A few years from now I suspect that companies will gradually give up more control in favor of moving more workloads to the public cloud as the public cloud vendors continue to add more features focused on winning more enterprise and government business. The role of IT will shift toward integrating APIs and industry-specific clouds and away from building large amounts of code internally.

At the end of the day, it all comes down to architecture. Understand the business requirements first and foremost. Map the right cloud service models and deployment models to the business needs. Build what is core to the business and leverage PaaS and SaaS solutions for everything else. Make sure the architecture addresses the different strategies in this book: auditing, data, security, logging, SLAs, monitoring, disaster recovery, DevOps, and organizational impacts. And finally, have fun and enjoy the ride!

INDEX

Note: Page numbers in *italics* indicate figures and tables.